Mary Quee
in Staffordshire

Mary Queen of Scots in Staffordshire

The plots & the plotters

Trevor Fisher

YouCaxton Publications
Oxford & Shrewsbury

Dedication

For my mother, Mrs Julia Fisher, and to Lady Antonia Fraser. When my mother was bedridden towards the end of her life, she liked reading history. Hearing about the best selling biography of the Scottish Queen which Lady Antonia Fraser had published, she decided to read it. Having had very little historical education, she struggled with some of the political issues. She interrogated me, expected me as a history graduate to have all the answers, and would not take "it's not my period" as a response. I had to research the conflicted life of Mary Stuart. Though my mother passed away many years ago, she remains the inspiration and provocation behind this book. Lady Fraser's book is the bedrock for my continuing study.

Acknowledgements

The author wishes to thank Netta Cartwright, Elaine Henshaw and Dr Nigel Tringham for help and advice on this project, gratefully acknowledged. Any remaining errors are the responsibility of the author.

PREFACE

Beyond the Celebrity image

Mary Stuart - famous as Mary Queen of Scots - is a celebrity figure though more than four centuries have passed since her execution.[1] The 2018 film, based on John Guy's 2004 biography, mainly showed her time in Scotland, ending with a meeting with her cousin Elizabeth 1 which never actually happened. This study deals with aspects of her life after she stopped being the Scottish Queen. She lived longer in England than Scotland, and was a captive of the English queen for 19 years in the Midland counties of Staffordshire, Derbyshire, South Yorkshire and Northamptonshire. Her history is legendary and yet even the best biographies leave much unexplained.

Much of the story is familiar, especially from the excellent biographies of Antonia Fraser and John Guy, though they tend to sympathise with a personality whose career has been described as "a study in failure". The Scottish writer, Jenny Wormald, based this judgement on a study of the Queen's time in Scotland.[2] Since she wrote this thirty years ago, research has filled in many issues relating to her flight to England and her activity while captive, but her time in the English provinces is less focussed than court intrigue. The plots which sought to release her from that captivity, specifically over her time in Staffordshire, often see her as victim and underestimate her ability to plot to become free. While close confined by soldiers, she was nevertheless still able to plot and her plotting, in secret and using coded letters, creating acute tension with her cousin, Queen Elizabeth.

For her time in Staffordshire, historical research has left major gaps affecting particularly the Earls revolt of 1569 which both Fraser and Guy dismiss as unimportant, and the lead up to the Babington plot in 1586, where Mary was misled by what I call the "Brewers Sting", which could only have taken place in Staffordshire. Historians find it easy to chart court intrigue and the domestic life of Mary and her party, but even obvious paradoxes of her treatment in the provinces are rarely explored. For example, it is well known that Tutbury Castle damaged her health, but when she was moved to Chartley by her notorious jailer Amyas Paulet, she recovered yet it proved fatal to her cause.

Mary did not understand the challenges she faced till she passed through the grim entrance of Tutbury and realised she was prisoner.

*This book outlines what the challenges were, how they came to be, and why despite the remoteness of the County, Staffordshire played a crucial role at crucial times in the story of Mary Stuart in England. Her party and her jailers deserve more than walk on, caricature parts. Staffordshire provided a stage and interpreting Mary as victim is at best a half truth. The county is a setting for a very dark story more often romanticised than closely studied - Mary in Staffordshire.

The grim entrance of Tutbury Castle

Contents

Introduction

One Day in Tixall[3]

On 11 August 1586, Mary Queen of Scots, the prisoner of Elizabeth 1, was invited by her jailer, Sir Amyas Paulet, to attend a deer hunt on the estate of Sir Walter Aston at Tixall in Staffordshire. The invitation was unusual since Paulet, a hard line puritan, was hostile to entertainment, especially for Mary and her servants. But Mary's current prison - the Manor House at Chartley four miles away - was due a belated spring clean. As Mary had recovered from illness a trip to Tixall near the former Royal Forest of Cannock Chase was now possible.

Mary embraced the chance of much needed exercise and an outlet for the growing optimism she was feeling. After many years she believed she was on the verge of release from what she saw as unjustified imprisonment. Elizabeth 1 had failed to help her regain the Scottish throne Mary had lost to rebels, and refused to name a successor for when she died while keeping Mary under lock and key. Mary - who was Elizabeth's cousin -believed there was only one possible successor - herself. No one denied she was next in line to take the throne. But while nine years younger than Elizabeth the chances of the Protestant government allowing her as a Catholic to become English Queen had been remote. Mary had never been prepared to wait anyway.

Mary had decided long ago to help fate on its way, and had spent the last decade and a half plotting to oust Elizabeth and take the throne after the English Queen had been killed. This now seemed within her grasp. She was conspiring with Anthony Babington and a group of Catholic plotters to have the Queen murdered, spark a Catholic rebellion, and take power. The plot was foolproof - or so she thought - and she waited for the overdue news of Elizabeth's death and the arrival of a force of Catholic rebels to overpower Paulet and her guards. A deer hunt on a summer's day would provide light relief while waiting.

Tixall Gatehouse

Mary saw a group of horsemen on the horizon and thought the moment had come. She awaited the inevitable confrontation as Catholic insurgents overpowered Protestant soldiers. To her suprise the captain of the horsemen spoke with Paulet and then approached her with shocking news. She was being arrested on a charge of plotting to kill Elizabeth. He was a government officer with instructions to put her and her servants under armed guard until her trial.

Mary blustered and ordered her servants to defend her, but Elizabeth's men drew loaded pistols and disarmed them. Mary was then taken to Tixall House for a fortnight away from Chartley Manor - its cleaning being a ruse to get her out while her quarters were searched - and after her rooms had been ransacked her papers were sent to Sir Francis Walsingham, Elizabeth's spycatcher. On August 25 she was taken back to Chartley before being put on trial at Fotheringhay. The Elizabeth's advisors in the English government wanted her dead: she had been protected as their heir to the throne. But her son James had signed a separate treaty with the English and was now old enough to be a King. Mary was simply a risk which had to be removed.

So how had Mary come to be in Staffordshire, a backwater in the English midlands, in an isolated part of the county at a place - Chartley - which had little to show but a ruined castle, the half timbered manor house of the Devereux family, and the nearby house of the magistrate Walter Aston at Tixall? Despite other counties being used to contain the exiled Queen, Staffordshire had proved to be ideal to cater for the problems posed by Mary Stuart. This is a story which deserves to be told.

Part 1
The Long Road to Exile

Chapter 1

A Queen's Outlook

Mary Stuart is known as Queen of Scots but experiences in three countries shaped her outlook and behaviour - in fact she lived in Scotland less than in England and France.

She spent even more time in England - in prison - than anywhere else, 18 years, 8 months and 23 days including two short but decisive periods in Staffordshire. She was in and out of Tutbury Castle three times in 1569 and 1570, then back in January 1585 for a final spell in Tutbury before being moved to the manors of Chartley and Tixall for the final drama in 1586. Time in Staffordshire was the dramatic opening and closing of a long period of hopes raised but not fulfilled.

She inherited the throne at six days old and saw herself as a Queen by divine right, in Scotland and England by birth and France - briefly - by marriage. She left Scotland when only 5 years and 7 days old. She only lived in the land of her birth for 12 years and four months. Educated in France to be the wife of the Dauphin her childhood and teenage years established in her mind that she was destined to be Queen in three countries. Her outlook was always that of a monarch, however different the reality proved to be.

A Perfect Creature
Half Scottish and half French by birth, she was the daughter of the Scots King James V, and his second wife the French Mary of Guise. She was born on 7th or 8th December 1542, as her father's only legitimate heir, eight days before her father died. She had an

illegitimate half brother, the Earl of Moray/ Murray, who caused her serious problems as Queen, but no one denied she was the rightful monarch. She inherited the Scottish throne following her father's death when he lost the Battle of Solway Moss to the English. Through her Father, she also had a claim to the English throne - her grandmother, Margaret Tudor, was sister to Henry VIII, making Mary the cousin of Elizabeth Tudor, who became Queen Elizabeth 1 from 1558. If Elizabeth had no children, Mary was next in line. To Catholics, Mary was the real heir to the throne as Elizabeth was not legitimate - her mother Anne Boleyn was not married to Henry VIII in a Catholic ceremony as Henry had become a protestant.

After being crowned Queen at ten months she was always a political pawn. She was the target of Henry VIII's attempt to force a marriage to his son Edward to unite the two thrones, known as the 'Rough Wooing' - Henry sent an army which fought the Scots. Mary was hidden in a priory following the Scots defeat at the battle of Pinkie Cleugh in 1547 and the regent, the Earl of Arran, made a deal with the French to send her to France to marry the French heir. Mary had a claim to be Royal in three countries after 1558, but only the Scots throne was hers without argument.

An arranged dynastic marriage was always her destiny as she had to marry Royalty. Her father had married a Frenchwoman and her grandfather had married an English woman as the choice was either English or French royalty, but the Scots had refused the English marriage so France it would be. Mary would have learnt from her youngest age that it was her destiny to be a Queen. It is worth noting that Elizabeth Tudor never had this expectation. She was the third in line and both her siblings Edward and Mary, were expected to marry and produce heirs. Elizabeth had not expected to become Queen. Mary always saw it as her birthright - and yet unlike her cousin she was doomed to be an ex-Queen despite having two coronations.

She was sent to France while her mother stayed in Scotland to ensure the country would be in a fit state if Mary was to return. Mary had gained the poise and assurance which came from her Royal status even before arriving in France. When she boarded the ship taking her to France on July 29th 1548 a French observer noted she was "one of the most perfect creatures that ever was seen".[4] At age 5 she had gained the star quality which she would have to the day of her execution.

For the next decade she was taught speak and write in French - even at Chartley she would prefer to write in French and dictated to a French secretary. France gave her experience of a Renaissance court. This shaped her in three ways that Scotland would not have done, firstly in court politics, secondly observing an absolute monarchy, her intended husband the Dauphin, Francis, was being trained to be in total control, and thirdly as a player in international politics. One of her uncles was a Cardinal and a powerful figure within Roman Catholic politics, while France was challenging Spain to be the most powerful country in Europe.

Her role as a Royal Asset

Mary was promised to the Dauphin, but a marriage depended on conditions. The Scots parliament insisted on their Queen not simply handing over power to her husband on marriage and sent an eight strong deputation to ensure this. Before the marriage was agreed this was accepted but two days earlier the dominant powers at Court - Mary's two Guise uncles - had intervened. Guy writes "two mutually contradictory sets of undertakings were given".[5] The Scots commissioners signed documents guaranteeing Scottish independence. But the Scots did not know that the French agenda was control of England and Scotland, Mary having already signed documents to allow this.

By the first, if Mary died without issue then the French kings inherited her rights over the Scottish and English thrones. Secondly, if she died without heirs Scottish money went to France to pay for

French troops sent to Scotland to fight against England in previous wars and to pay for her education. Thirdly, any future agreement signed with the Scots would be null and void.[6] The documents signed with the Scots commissioners were thus worthless. This was a cynical power grab but Mary was only a 15 year old adolescent. With her uncles in charge of the secret documents she could not refuse to sign them. It was a sharp lesson in machiavellian politics.

Guy comments that her uncles were 'cold hearted, even cruel. To them Mary was a dynastic asset to be exploited, not an adopted daughter to be cherished'.[7] The Scots began to question French motives, even those who were Catholics - when the French demanded the Scottish Crown be sent over, the Catholic Duke of Chatelherault joined Protestants opposing sending the Crown to France, fearing it would never return. It became increasingly clear that Mary's mother was ruling Scotland on behalf of the French, so the Scots began a fight for independence against Mary's mother - at the end of October 1559 rebel lords removed Mary of Guise as Regent, starting a war with her French troops, and with help from the English defeated her forces. Protestants north and south of the border were learning to co-operate.

Emotional Turmoil

On April 24th 1558 Mary and Francis were married in a spectacular ceremony as befitted the second most powerful country in Europe - Mary was 15 and Francis 14. They had hardly made their vows when their world began to change. On 17th November 1558 Mary Tudor died at the age of 42 and the English throne was vacant again for the second time in six years. When Edward VI had died Catholics had been satisfied: Mary Tudor - Bloody Mary to the protestants- was good news to Catholics being the legitimate heir as Henry VIII had married her mother by Catholic rites, unlike Elizabeth's mother Anne Boleyn. The church did not accept Elizabeth as legitimate though the Pope had not yet excommunicated her. Mary Stuart was a Catholic and her Guise uncles rushed to promote her as the real heir to the English throne. This would be a claim that never left Mary. Neither Catholics nor protestants would ever forget Mary had a claim to the English throne.

But the claim was little more than propaganda, as the 25 year old Elizabeth was crowned and securely in power, and the Guise had to pull back when Henry II found Phillip II of Spain was trying to marry Elizabeth to replace Mary Tudor who had been his wife. Diplomacy could not make Mary Stuart English Queen, but she never abandoned her claim to the English throne and Elizabeth always refused to meet her in protest. The Treaty of Edinburgh which agreed France and England would withdraw troops from Scotland accepted Elizabeth as Queen - and Mary refused to sign the Treaty, but as her mother - legally the Regent - died on 11th June 1560 Mary had no power over events in Scotland.

Mary had already become Queen Consort when her husband became King following a tragedy. On 30th June 1559 Henry II aged 40 challenged a rival to a joust, was hit in the eye by his opponents lance, and died on 10th July. Francis at 16 was now King, his wife at 17 Queen of France. But the turning point of her life was about to occur, a second unexpected death which this time nothing had prepared her for and would end her time in France.

In November 1560 Francis became seriously ill. He went into a coma and died from brain seizures on 5th December. This was the turning point of Mary's life. Perhaps she had not loved her husband, but her life had been based on training to be Consort of the French King. Now the Crown passed to his 10 year old brother Charles and power to her mother in law Catherine de Medici. She had no place in the politics of France under a woman who had never liked her, and staying when her Guise relations were being squeezed out of the French court made little sense. The documents they had made her sign were no longer a guide to the future and French politicians would have no influence over events in Scotland now her mother was no longer Regent; the future of Scotland was in Scottish hands

Mary decided to return to her home country and finally become Queen of Scots. But she would take with her lessons she had learnt from her uncles, the dominant lesson being their belief that victory was everything. They had been masters of the dark arts of machiavellian politics. These Mary would never forget. She was naturally charming, but her skills in .power politics she had learned in France and would attempt to use in the very different countries of Scotland and England through to the final plotting with Babington at Chartley. But her skills were only useful if she had control. In Scotland she would have power at the beginning of her reign, or at least tolerance which gave her space to build a following.

Chapter 2

The Queen's Scottish downfall.

After the death of Francis, the Guise family lost control of French politics, so there was no future for Mary as a Dowager Queen. Over the rest of her life she never forgot France and M Greengrass comments "She remained for the rest of her life a French queen"- though this was only in her head. French politicians had no further use for her. She asked to be buried in Rheim in her final will, next to her Cardinal uncle Charles de Lorraine.[8] But while she was emotionally committed to France, the French experience did not define her. The next period of her life did.

She was 18 when she chose to return home. Scotland was now a different world from the one she left aged 5. The protestant Lords dominated parliament, French influence was in decline. The Treaty of Edinburgh agreed after the death of her Mother evacuated French troops from Scotland, along with English troops, and when signed on 6th July 1560 recognised Elizabeth as English monarch The Scottish parliament also enacted the Scottish Reformation and made the Catholic mass illegal. Mary would never accept these decisions but she would never be able to get enough troops or Scottish backers to control events.[9]

The Treaty was the first conflict of the reign, produced before Mary came to Scotland and without any contribution from her. Jenny Wormald comments that she spent 14 months doing nothing- "the unique spectacle of a monarch who made no attempt at all to impose her rule".[10] This is unfair - she did not know what to do. She was after all a teenager whose world had just been turned upside down. She could have stayed in France as Dowager Queen and not return to a realm where as a Catholic she was in a minority but bravely she made plans to return to Scotland.

She believed she had to trust her half brother, James Stuart, Earl of Moray (or Murray), who was protestant, but did not know who else to trust. Handling tension with England over the Treaty might have been helped had she met Elizabeth. The Scots ambassador d'Oysel in London requested a passport to allow Mary to pass through England, which could have led to her visiting London and meeting her cousin, Elizabeth initially refused because the treaty had not been signed and when she changed her mind Mary was already sailing north. The missed opportunity for the two Queens to meet was a game changer - they never met and their relationship remained based on correspondence, initially friendly but always frosty where signing the Treaty and being named as Elizabeth's heir were concerned. Elizabeth always reacted badly when anyone mentioned the succession to the English throne, but never contested Mary's right to succeed, making her attitude to Mary deeply enigmatic.

Elizabeth 's chief advisor William Cecil - later Lord Burghley - was deeply hostile to Mary as he was a Calvinist protestant sympathetic to the Scottish preacher John Knox. Cecil had no ability to stop Mary's legal right to inherit so hoped that Elizabeth would marry and provide an heir writing his hope "God send our mistress a husband, and by him a son, that we may hope that our posterity shall have a masculine succession".[11] Elizabeth's refusal to marry placed Mary top of his list of problems.

Before Mary left France and while still seeking out Scottish politicians she could rely on, at some point in autumn of 1560 she met James Hepburn in Paris, Earl of Bothwell, Lord High Admiral, who made an indelible impression, though not all were favourable to him. The English Ambassador Nicholas Throckmorton reported the Earl was "a rash and hazardous young man".[12] Sadly Mary had appalling judgement of men, and Bothwell would seriously damage her life and reputation.

English diplomats in France urged Mary to ratify the Treaty of Edinburgh and accept Elizabeth was English Queen. Mary left the Treaty unsigned, travelling to Scotland by sea so symbolically avoiding English soil. She arrived in Scotland on August 19th 1561, aged 18 years and 8 months, landing in the port of Leith.

Mary Stuart on the throne

Although Mary was politically inexperienced, and a Catholic in a land increasingly Protestant, she made a good start. Even the hostility of charismatic preacher John Knox who played on sexism in his tract *"The First Blast of the Trumpet Against the Monstrous Regiment of Women",* had little immediate effect. Her authority was not questioned because she was a woman. Overall she started well, declaring religious tolerance, though her Catholicism was a problem which Knox played on.

The political climate in Scotland was marred by considerable violence, but she was welcomed on her return as being the rightful monarch and many hoped she might heal some of the bitter factional disputes between clans and politicians. This was overoptomistic and in 1565 relations broke down with her half brother over her planned marriage to a Catholic nobleman with English heritage Lord Darnley. Moray claimed this would reinforce the Catholic religion in Scotland, but Moray was seen as seeking power through his rebellion and Mary had no choice but to go to battle. Mary raised five times the number of troops as her half brother and chased him around and out of the country in what was known as the Chaseabout raid. Always courageous, she personally led troops to fight and had her own steel helmet.

The English were more concerned that the marriage strengthened Mary's claim to the English throne, both bride and groom being related to Elizabeth 1 as cousins, so children born to the couple would have an even stronger claim to the English throne than they did individually. The child of the marriage, James Stuart, did indeed become king of both countries After the Chaseabout Raid his future uncle James Stuart, Earl of Moray fled to England, where Elizabeth read him a lecture against rebellion. Mary drew from this the mistaken conclusion she could rely on Elizabeth for support against rebels. In the turmoil following the breakdown of the marriage Moray was allowed back into Scotland but was never reconciled with his sister - and Elizabeth was not concerned about his rebellion whatever she said, support for monarchy not having any effect when religion became the issue.

Sadly the marriage was the first of Mary's disasterous mistakes. Darnley was a pretty boy who was good in bed, but he was also a violent, drunken, bi-sexual psychopath. Guy describes him as '"the depraved and dangerously conspiratorial Darnley".[13] Obviously Mary did not know this when they married, but soon found out. Darnley did the business required of a royal husband - he got her pregnant, solving the problem of the succession to the throne, but the marriage broke down and he was banned from Mary's bed - with results that triggered a scandal echoing across Europe.

Darnley assumed Mary was having an affair with her secretary, Rizzio, who spent much free time with her. A group of Darnley's friends agreed to back him up in an attack on Rizzio, the mob broke into Mary's private rooms stabbing Rizzio to death, dragging him away from Mary as he clung to her skirt. She showed considerable courage in facing up to Darnley's violence when six months pregnant, and he fled to Glasgow.[14] There was a pause in the conflict as Mary prepared for her confinement, and the Queen gave birth three months later, James her son arriving on 19th June 1566. Darnley did not attend his son's christening showing the relationship was profoundly tense. [15]

There was an apparent reconciliation and Mary visited Darnley in Glasgow and took Darnley back to Edinburgh - Antonia Fraser commenting "it seemed safer for herself and her child to have him lodged in Edinburgh"[16] - but there may have been more to transferring Darnley to Edinburgh than Royal self preservation. Darnley was blown up at his lodgings in Kirk o Fields, and then strangled. The murder was blamed on the Earl of Bothwell, and Mary was widely condemned for her handling of the murder investigation. The trial of Bothwell was a farce. The Earl of Lennox - Darnley's father -stayed away. Bothwell had 4000 troops in the City. Darnley's murder remains controversial and Mary may not have known what was being planned. But she failed to find out who killed her husband.

This was a public relations disaster. Jenny Wormald probably assesses public opinion in a violent society correctly in arguing "Mary could have continued her reign, free of the albatross (Darnley TF) because that was what people wanted..."[17] as long as she avoided appearing to condone murder, and this she did not do. Even the very sympathetic John Guy writing this "tarnished her reputation, and rightly so. She made no serious attempt to bring Darnley's killers to justice".[18] While this was perhaps negligence, her relationship with Bothwell became toxic, the third scandal grew out of this and destroyed any credibility she had.

The protestants, incited by the puritan preacher John Knox, already detested a person they regarded as morally unfit, but, Catholics were equally shocked and April was for her the cruellest month, when her behaviour destroyed any moral standing she had left. On April 4th Mary witnessed Bothwell attack an old man who had worked for Darnley and wanted charity as he was destitute. Bothwell assaulted him so severely he died two hours later. He was above the law, and saw his trial for murder of Darnley as a formality, his troops in Edinburgh ensuring this was the case. Mary had now seen the dark side of the man she would see acquitted of her second husband's murder and take as her third.[19] Scottish public opinion now swung against her. The Earl of Mar refused to hand over her ten month old son James when he was due to return him after the traditional Scottish period of foster care. Mary was only allowed into the nursery with two female attendants, the Queen could not take male servants along to ensure she could not take James away with her. Mary last saw her son on April 21st 1567 aged 10 months. Mary's tolerance of Bothwell meant she would never see James again. She was considered unfit to be a mother

The scandal intensified when despite Bothwell still being accused of Darnley's murder, Mary married him even though he was both extremely violent and a protestant. Mary claimed Bothwell had raped her, and she had no choice but to marry him as he was the father of her unborn twins. This argument had no credibility, and the nobles went to war against the couple. The confrontation at Carberry Hill on July 15th 1567 was farcical - no battle took place as Bothwell had few troops and was allowed safe passage to avoid bloodshed. Mary never saw him again - they were a married couple just five weeks. After two months in which he tried to find men to fight for him, failing for men saw him as tainted goods and would not risk their lives for him, Bothwell fled the country, leaving Mary to be captive and forced to abdicate.[20]

After Bothwell

Mary was imprisoned in the castle at Loch Leven, the considerable brutality used to make her sign the abdication document caused her to miscarry her twins. This treatment was both unjust and unwise, creating sympathy for her and allowing her one last episode as a ruler. She was always charismatic and had loyal supporters among those who met her and fell under her spell. Residents in the prison that the castle on Loch Leven had become helped her escape. She went to Hamilton where her supporters rallied while her half brother James Stuart, Earl of Moray gathered troops. When the two sides met in battle at Langside outside Glasgow the result, Guy said, "appeared a foregone conclusion"[21] as her troops outnumbered those of Moray by a third. But Moray's troops fought harder, Lord Argyll in charge of Mary's army collapsed in a fit, and fighting was over in three quarters of an hour.

The battle on 13th May 1568 was her last act as Queen in Scotland. Mary watched her defeat from a hill, panicked and made her escape taking only the clothes she stood up in. She hoped writing a letter to Elizabeth 1 in England asking for support and sending back a ring Elizabeth had given to her in 1563 as a token of friendship would provide a way forward. She crossed over into England hoping to return with English support. Inquests on her reign have never ceased.

The sympathetic John Guy puts her decision to leave Scotland as "A catastrophic mistake.[22] It precipitated a crisis in England, where it was feared that the northern and still overwhelmingly Catholic counties would rise in her support, leading to civil war in both countries". This is entirely correct. In summer 1568 Elizabeth had no feeling of political insecurity. Once Mary had arrived, uneasy lay the head that wore the crown, and what happened to Mary in England was the predictable result of not seeing the effect of her religion on an insecure protestant regime. In Scotland Mary had squandered support across both religions. In England she would be standard bearer for only one.

It is undeniable Mary had a very difficult hand to play when she returned aged only 18. The Puritan preacher John Knox was railing at "The monstrous regiment of women", but that attack points to an important fact. It was a man's world, but there were several important women rulers in the sixteenth century and all did better than Mary. Jenny Wormald [23] points to Mary of Guise (Mary Stuart's own mother), Catherine de Medici, Mary of Hungary, Margaret of Parma and Mary Tudor. Even the latter - England's 'bloody Mary' did better than Mary Stuart and died in her own bed. Above all there is Elizabeth 1, the most successful of them all. Mary Stuart had at the very least played her hand badly. What would now happen would be decided by others. She had lost control of her fate.

Part 2
The Exiled Queen

Chapter 3

1568 - Arrival in England

The Queen had no plan of escape and had no transport to sail back to France, so took a fishing boat crossing the Solway Firth for England. She was taken to Carlisle where Lord Scrope, government official for the northern counties and Sir Francis Knollys, Elizabeth's roving representative, travelled to make sure she was under Royal control. The exile arrived in England expecting the English to lend her an army to regain the Scottish throne. Elizabeth, who was totally opposed to rebels overthrowing monarchs, had made statements to this effect. But Mary, taking rhetoric at face value, underestimated how weak she was asking a Protestant Queen to support her as a Catholic against Protestant lords.

Mary showed tunnel vision which stopped her seeing the problems she would face in England. Her belief that Elizabeth would put her back on the throne lasted at least two and a half years, she was negotiating with the Secretary of State Cecil as late as September 1570, though at the same time negotiating with the Spanish and French as best she could. Antonia Fraser comments that her preference was always for asolution with a great power backing and "at the head of her list of major powers who she thought would help her was still Elizabeth -whom Mary still hoped would achieve her restoration to Scotland in the end".[24] The illusion Elizabeth would aid her stemmed from her core belief that monarchs helped monarchs. The next two decades would put this to the test.

After long conversations with Francis Knollys, her first guardian - really jailer - the English government was in little doubt she had only one aim. He reported that she was in fighting spirit and "in respect of victory, wealth and all things seem to her contempible and vile". Black has Knollys saying "what she most thirsteth after is victory... (over the rebels led by James Stuart Earl of Moray or Murray - her half brother - now Regent in charge of her son James).[25] From the moment she was born, she was told she was destined to rule. That the people who mattered in Scotland and England did not agree she never seemed to understand or see as an issue.

Her Guise Uncles in France were effective but limited teachers. Mary was driven by the achievement of power and the defeat of anyone and anything that stood in the way. Throughout her time in England the belief in absolute monarchy was her guiding star, making her behaviour rigid and reinforcing the Scottish protestant belief no agreement would ever lead to a compromise. She never understood that in England and Scotland, unlike France which was an absolute monarchy, the crowned head would always need to take public opinion - at least among the nobility - into account rather than making arbitrary decisions expecting automatic support. Her appeals internationally fell on deaf ears.

The months of 1568 after her arrival left her in limbo. She was moved from Carlisle, a town where an invasion force could be mobilised, to Lord Scrope's Bolton Castle in Wensleydale in North Yorkshire. This according to John Guy was comfortable - it even had primitive central heating and Lady Scrope was a generous hostess. It was clear from the start her status as Queen was preserved. But this was still house arrest in an isolated valley with no towns nearby, possibly a factor as it would be in moving her to Chartley in the closing stages of her time in England.

Mary was optomistic about Elizabeth's support, knowing Elizabeth was always hostile to rebels against annointed monarchs, but Mary was seriously controversial. Armed backing had to wait till she was cleared of being part of the plot to murder her husband Darnley. The Scots lords claimed she was involved and the allegations meant English support was suspended till the charges of involvement in the murder of Darnley were eliminated. The English government set up an inquiry with Mary and her accusers presenting their evidence. But in defiance of all fairness, Mary had to operate via representatives - she was confined to Bolton.

Elizabeth promised backing if Mary was proved innocent - writing, "once honourably acquitted of this crime, I swear to you before God that among all worldly pleasures THAT will hold the first rank".[26] Mary was furious when not allowed to attend to answer the charges against her. Her half brother James Stuart was allowed to attend and he would bring as evidence the Casket Letters which became controversial as Mary claimed they were faked. Moray - James Stuart - led a protestant government. Protestant England supported their co-religionists. And all were aware the long standing 'Auld Alliance' of Scots and French was a key problem for English foreign policy. Mary as a former French Queen could revive that Alliance if she were the Scottish Queen. Even if Mary was declared innocent, she could not go back to Scotland, though the inquiry focussed on whether this was the issue.

The Inquiry began in York on October 4th 1568[27] led by the Duke of Norfolk, England's premier aristocrat, plus the veteran diplomat Sir Ralph Sadler, and the Earl of Sussex. On 11th October Moray put the casket letters in as evidence, letters allegedly from Mary confirming her role in the Darnley murder. Discussion became bogged down on whether they were genuine. Elizabeth moved the inquiry to Westminster, but it made little more progress with an enlarged membership. Sussex[28] wrote that if Mary appeared and denied the letters she would have to be acquitted - so she could not appear. Norfolk wrote he was 'shocked' by the letters. But shock perhaps that they had been produced when Mary could not respond? Norfolk was beginning to be personally involved in the affairs of the Queen.

Fraser suggests that Mary's advisors, William Maitland (political secretary) and Catholic Bishop John Leslie proposed that Norfolk should marry Mary, giving him a powerful incentive to have her declared innocent.[29] This had little immediate impact, but had long term consequences for the Duke. But Norfolk was only one voice. Clearing Mary meant releasing Mary. This was far too dangerous- the Scots Lords were never interested in having her back- and allowing her to go to a Catholic power would unleash dangerous possibilities - backed by a Foreign Catholic army she would be a threat to Scotland and England, and politicians in both countries would take no risks with the exiled Queen. Even if she did not go back to Scotland she could not be freed to go free to go back to France - the fear of a French backed regime and the Auld Alliance back was ever present. Fraser says that before the Westminster proceedings opened on November 25th Moray was received by Elizabeth - she never met Mary.[30] Protestantism and Real Politik meant the door was closed.

But Elizabeth did not take the Casket letters at face value. She drew back when condemning an annointed monarch, and accepting the letters as genuine would mean this. By January 1569 the verdict was announced as 'not proven'.

A Marriage Plot

Meanwhile as the inquiry ground towards its not proven verdict, a relationship with Thomas Howard Duke of Norfolk was developing even though they may never have actually met. By an accident of fate, Mary at Bolton Castle had found herself counselled by the Duke of Norfolk's sister, and Lady Scope knew her brother wished to marry Mary. Norfolk was vastly ambitious and was eager to marry a Queen- as he had been recently widowed he was looking for a wife. Mary was also interested in a match with a Duke which could strengthen her claim to the English throne. Divorce from the protestant Bothwell was requested from the Catholic church though in practice an annulment was never granted. But in 1568 everything seemed possible. Howard was the only Duke in England, was Elizabeth's cousin, and a marriage looked very attractive.

Although they only corresponded - Antonia Fraser thought they never met at all- and Guy can find only one meeting - Mary wrote him love letters, one ending "Your own faithful till death, Queen of Scots, My Norfolk."[31] The Duke sent her a diamond ring which she later wore at her trial. The idea of their marriage attracted support from other aristocrats who saw the chance to keep Mary under an aristocratic thumb. But there was a fly in the ointment. Elizabeth was kept in the dark as she would inevitably see Mary as a threat. Both the Duke and the Queen were her cousins. Children of the marriage would make her look redundant.

Norfolk was vital to Elizabeth's government and until Mary arrived was a trusted pillar of a seemingly secure regime The Spanish Ambassador de Silva reported in July 1568 on a trip to Reading that Eliabeth "...was received everywhere with great acclamations...". He noted that she even took up food and drink without waiting for a taster to check for signs of poison.[32] This was a golden age - in the south of England, not the Catholic north. The Queen only went north of the Trent twice in her reign, to Staffordshire - including Chartley - and Lincolnshire, where she went to Gainsborough. In the first decade of her reign religious tensions were contained.

Elizabeth had no reason to fear challenges in the summer of 1568, but when Mary arrived in England that May a cloud came over the horizon starting four years of crisis 1568-72 which some historians think ended with the execution of Norfolk for high treason. Nevertheless Elizabeth's relationship with Norfolk was sound when Mary arrived and he was the obvious leader of the inquiry into the inquiry into Darnley's murder being a Protestant, if not strongly of the faith - the Howards would revert to being Catholics as they are to this day.

That summer the Queen was hearing rumours of a relationship. She critically examined Norfolk about these and he replied.[33] "Should I seek to marry her, being so wicked a woman, such a notorious adulteress and murderer?". And being well aware Mary had never abandoned her claim to be English Queen, he added a proposal "Might that justly charge me with seeking the crown from your head". Clearly the case, but the rumours kept coming and the Queen asked him a little later What news was abroad? He had none. "No?" she replied, "You come from London and have no news of a marriage?" He was silent. His marriage plans were not to be discussed. But he was now suspected of operating a hidden agenda, and this was to become a toxic issue.

Mary was worried and Bishop Ross asked Norfolk on her behalf what would happen if Elizabeth forced his hand. He replied "There would be no noblemen in England accept that charge at her command, for he knew their whole minds, especially those in the north, who would assist him...."[34] He said this in summer 1569, but his whole attitude to the marriage was based on having support from his fellow nobles. This support melted away when Elizabeth found out what was planned.

By the end of 1568 the inquiry ground to a halt. Mary could not be acquitted - but she could not be convicted either. She could not be supported for the Scottish throne as not proved innocent of involvement in murder, nor allowed to go to Europe where she could be used in foreign plots. English politicians feared her role in making England a nut in a political nut cracker by reviving the Auld Alliance of Scotland and France - though the English were not aware the Medici government in France was losing interest in supporting their former Queen. Spain was already in 1568 the coming threat.

The Inquiry was declared by Elizabeth on January 10th 1569 to have failed to come to a decision on Mary's role in the murder of Darnley, but the comfortable surroundings of Bolton castle were barred to her. It was too far north for comfort and too obviously in a Catholic area, so she was moved to a fortress overlooking the midland plain. On January 26th 1569 Mary began the journey south to the grim fortress of Tutbury in Staffordshire.

Chapter 4

1569 Tutbury a castle and prison

Mary arrived at Tutbury on February 3rd 1569 and realised for the first time that she was a captive. On a bleak winters day the place itself provided a very unpleasant shock. Compared to the comfortable setting of Bolton Castle, this grim mediaeval fortress with no sympathetic aristocratic company was a brutal wake up call. The castle was owned by the Crown but placed in the charge of George Talbot, Earl of Shrewsbury, a very wealthy nobleman. He owned 7 mansions all of which were more palatial than the ancient castle overlooking the River Dove which was being used to house the Royal Stud.

The horses were kept in the Castle Park and not the castle itself, so Mary was not sharing her living space, nevertheless the contrast between Bolton, Carlisle Castle and the luxurious houses of Scotland and France she had known giving a stark reminder of how low Mary had fallen. Tutbury had known high ranking people, notably John of Gaunt, but by 1569 it was a decaying relic of mediaeval society.

Of all the places Mary was imprisoned, Tutbury was the place she hated most. It had been recently repaired but was extremely damp and a large marsh under the walls sent up fumes which were worsened by the sewers which drained into the marsh - part of military life for mediaeval soldiers perhaps but for someone suffering Mary's illnesses it posed potentially lethal threats to her health. Shrewsbury found better accommodation when he was able to but in the first year she was there political unrest meant she was moved out twice and back in response to escalating fears of plots to release her. The government's priority was to block rescue attempts.

On this basis, the castle ticked all the boxes. Located on a hill far from the Catholic North, and distant from coastal ports where a foreign army might land to free the exile, an army would be needed to break its defences. It is believed that the village of Etwall, five miles away, is the place in England furthest from the coast. The living conditions were spartan, with little furniture until Elizabeth ordered beds, bedding and carpets, but nothing could relieve the chill in winter, dry out the damp walls, or cure the problems with stinking drains. The castle was substantial, almost a small village unlike the bare enclosure of today, and large enough to accommodate a large party, which Mary expected.

There was a lack of water for the launderesses to work and limited room for other minor servants and these workers had to stay in the town of Tutbury. Their passage in and out was a way for secret correspondence to enter and leave the castle, These issues plus the illnesses the Queen suffered when at Tutbury meant Shrewsbury was constantly looking for better lodgings for her . But when there were serious concerns about security the isolated and easily defended castle was always the final option.

Within days of entering the mediaeval walls, Mary Stuart was ill in bed with rheumatism and a fever. She had hardly recovered when she suffered severe abdominal pains, and in early spring Shrewsbury wrote to Cecil that she suffered from "grief of the spleen" and moved her to his house at Wingfield in nearby Derbyshire and then to his wife Bess of Hardwick's house at Chatsworth - inherited from her second husband Sir William Cavendish and owned by the Cavendish family to this day - when Wingfield was being cleaned. Moving the inhabitants wholesale out of a Tudor house was the only way to clean and sanitise it in the Sixteenth Century. Then with Catholic plots developing in the autumn of 1569 she was moved back to Tutbury on September 21st. The castle was secure, but needed reinforcements in a crisis. Whether Shrewsbury was the man for a military crisis was to be debated in the Privy council.

The domestic arrangements

Wherever she was kept, Mary behaved as a Queen, and the fiction she was a 'guest' of Elizabeth allowed considerable priveleges. A visitor to Tutbury in February 1569, the protestant Nicholas White reported to Cecil, Elizabeth's secretary of state, (Lord Burghley from 1571) "She hath withal an alluring grace, a pretty Scotch accent, and a searching wit, clouded with mildness. Fame might move some to relieve her, and glory might stir others to adventure much for her sake". He reported that she had two main rooms, a privy room and a 'presence room' which doubled as a dining room.[35] Guy concludes that "White's report shows how civilised and luxurious Mary's surroundings were. And yet they were still a prison"[36] with guards patrolling outside. The report also confirmed the impression Mary made of charm and beauty as even her puritan critics accepted - John Knox had said when she opened the Scottish parliament she had "Vox Dianae! The voice of a goddess... was there ever orator spake so properly and so sweetly!".[37] The impact she made was always considerable, and she was always a Queen whatever happened.

The exiled Queen came to Tutbury as Royalty in exile -she maintained what Fraser calls a 'mimic court'[38] and her much prized cloth of state was on the wall, symbol of her Royal status. She slept in a state bed whose linen was changed every day.[39] She had her own cook, partly because of her fear of poisoning. In this first period, when she was treated with kid gloves, the meals always had two courses, of 16 dishes each, twice a day -a total of 64 dishes - though she rarely had company. She ate off silver plates and drank out of crystal glassware. Mary's women were allowed nine dishes, her secretaries seven or eight, and the lesser servants and families consumed the left overs.

She had always had a close relationship with women friends, notably the Four Maries who had accompanied her to France to be educated.[40] One stayed with her till 1585, Mary Seton (or Seaton), the only one unmarried, accompanied her from Scotland and knew Christopher Norton, son of the rebel of 1569 Richard Norton. The Norton family were central to the Earls Rebellion of autumn 1569 and the father was a key plotter who may have entertained the exiled Queen as she passed through Yorkshire on the way to Tutbury. Antonia Fraser's curt comment that Christopher "may have fallen in love with her, although he was unfortunately executed at the time of the northern rising"[41] hardly scratches the surface. He suffered the death of a traitor, and hanging, drawing and quartering did not happen because of his interest in Mary Seton. He may have found himself a post at Wingfield in summer 1569 to be close to her, but it is likely he was part of a plot to release her which by that summer Mary had no interest in pursuing. The coincidence is too easily overlooked. Mary Seton was a skilled hairdresser, when she went to France to retire Mary Stuart's hair suffered as a result. At her execution her hair was grey: the executioner held her severed head but grasped a wig: the head fell to the ground.

The exiled Queen had 16 servants when she first arrived, but the number later reached three figures till reduced as a security measure and rose and fell according to the level of threat. She refused to wear any clothes but her own and when she arrived in England Knollys sent to Loch Leven for the wardrobe she had left behind when she escaped, receiving five cartloads and four horse loads. A year later she had bought so many replacements she needed thirty carts to move her personal effects when she moved from place to place.[42] She was able to follow the Catholic faith under Shrewsbury's regime, Fraser who as a Catholic was attuned to religious issues noted one Sir John Morton in her menage was a priest[43] - other priests were able to enter Tutbury even under Ralph Sadler much later which is one reason in the end the government brought in a regime of rigid strictness.

She corresponded extensively, but suffered from loneliness and particularly the neglect of her son. Correspondence with her son James never reached him as the Regents who ran the Scottish government stopped her letters to prevent plots against the Scottish government. Her attempts to maintain contact failed and not till he was 18 did he write to her. He never had any interest in his mother's plan for a joint monarchy and until his late teens a council of nobles ran the Scottish government and they would not pass on birthday presents his mother sent to Scotland.

In these early years, Mary had luxuries including fine silks and gold thread for embroidery, which marriage, and the works survive as evidence of her attitudes and skills. The cloth of state had the motto 'in my end is my beginning' along with the symbol of the Phoenix which had been used by her mother, and which patently meant overcoming serious obstacles- White did not understand this, though it is less obscure than other symbols used by Mary.

For example a cushion sent to the Duke of Norfolk in 1570 and perhaps done at Tutbury had the hand of Godwith a pruning hook, cutting off the unfruitful branches from a vine with the motto VIRESCIT VULNERE VIRTUS- 'virtue flourishes by wounding' - which Gareth Williams believes means cutting away the unfruitful Elizabeth "indicating Mary's willingness to plot against Elizabeth even at this early date".[44] While this is speculative, it is far from impossible. If this was indeed 1570 and after the crushing of the Northern Rebellion this ties in with support for the Ridolfi plot, developing in that year. In 1569 Mary was aware of plots for both an armed invasion from abroad and a marriage. Mary favoured the marriage: she wanted to be released to live in luxury, violence being very much a second choice if she had any say in the matter.

Plots, rebels and a marriage plan

On arrival in England, Mary courted international support for rebellion. The new Spanish Ambassador de Spes appointed in July 1568 had seen the possibility of a coup to release her from Bolton and "even raise a revolt against this Queen" - Spain being the most powerful Catholic Nation in Europe and Philip II the King having been married to Mary Tudor, the prospects of overturning the Protestant church were always being explored. In January 1569 Mary sent a message to de Spes that "If his master would help me, I shall be Queen of England in three months, and mass shall be said all over the country".[45] De Spes believed her but the Spanish government ignored him. In 1569 it remained the case that Catholics had no approval from the Church for killing Elizabeth. Neither the Spanish nor French would back Mary in 1569, and both countries had other priorities than invading England.

More importantly, when Mary arrived in Tutbury on February 3rd 1569 the shock of realising she was now a prisoner in an almost impregnable fortress changed her perpective. She was politically astute enough to realise that Tutbury was so securely built that it would make a successful release depend on a sizeable army, she switched her hopes to a possible marriage to secure her priority - release from imprisonment. Nevertheless, Mary could not help being a Catholic figurehead. Antonia Fraser is on strong ground in arguing that "Mary was therefore a catalyst rather than a chief conspirator in the two plots which followed".[46] She had agreed to marry Thomas Howard, and in the spring gave no encouragement to .plots to release her, believing a well placed marriage was the best route to securing her freedom. Aristocrats were well placed to support her marriage in the early part of 1569

She cultivated her relationship with Shrewsbury and Bess and enjoyed the summer climate in Derbyshire. At Chatsworth there is still an easily guarded bower which is said to have been used by her to take the air.

The tangled web in the summer of 1569

Mary hoped for a diplomatic solution and her release, and this was also Elizabeth's priority as long as no threat to her throne developed. Elizabeth wanted to secure a settlement and drew up three proposals in summer 1569 - Mary to abdicate and live in England, return to Scotland and rule jointly with James, though he was too young to make decisions, or return as Queen with conditions to safeguard the protestants. Mary favoured returning as queen, but the Scots nobles voting 40-9 in Perth in July not to have her back under any conditions closed that door.[47] The view that Elizabeth wanted Mary imprisoned in England has to take into account the talks in mid summer 1569 to find a way out for both Mary and Elizabeth which show a clear desire to release her. But the cleft stick in which Elizabeth found herself since May arrived uninvited was now closing like a vice. Elizabeth did not want to keep Mary, but could only allow her back to Scotland if the protestant Lords could accommodate her in a political settlement. They could not so Mary would remain in prison.

Elizabeth was increasingly unsettled by rumours of the marriage plan and Catholic discontent in the North of England. Indications of a wider Catholic conspiracy of which the Norfolk marriage was only a part were developing. Assessing the growing risk was impossible as there was no secret service, but tension was growing . The fact that Mary had left Tutbury for Shrewsbury's palatial but unfortified house at Wingfield became an issue. Chatsworth and WIngfield during the summer were acceptable locations as Mary had been gravely ill. But with rebellion in the air, these suddenly came to be dangerously vulnerable.

The focus of historians has always been on the Norfolk marriage and court conspiracy - court intrigues leave many records. But planning for armed rebellion is treason and leaves few records. Three lords in the North - the Earls of Northumberland and Westmorland, and Lord Dacre - were plotting, pushed by gentry

Catholic supporters. We know that the Norton family were leading the way - and that both Norfolk and Mary Stuart knew what was being talked about. One of Norfolk's sisters was married to the Earl of Westmorland - and Thomas Howard, the premiere Duke, was involved in a court case with Leonard Dacre. The small aristocratic circle in which everyone knew everyone else meant secrets were impossible to keep. North of the Trent however meetings were kept under wraps but government agents in the north picked up rumours, and it was obvious moving the Queen to Tutbury was wise.

By September 1569 there was a serious crisis facing Elizabeth Tudor.. There was no choice but to return the exile to Tutbury whatever Mary felt about the place and she was taken back on September 21st to the one place known to be secure. But how secure?

Mary knew something about a planned rebellion and wrote her disapproval. She was not centrally involved in the machinations though Shrewsbury could never check what she was doing. It is easy therefore to argue events had little do with her. All the insecurities of a government not fully in control of the country the further north its operatives travelled from London focussed on Mary Stuart. She could plead innocence but a closer look at the evidence suggests that locked away though she was, she was still the key to what happened.

Chapter 5

Tutbury and the Earls Revolt

By the summer of 1569, Mary Stuart found herself caught up in two plots, the marriage plot and the Catholic rebellion only one of which she endorsed- the marriage plot. Locked away in the charge of the Earl of Shrewsbury, her priority was to get released. A rebellion was too a high a risk. A marriage would however take her out of captivity. How much emotional commitment she really had to the Duke of Norfolk is obscure despite affectionate letters. In August 1571 Mary's advisor, John Leslie (Bishop of Ross TF) told the Spanish Ambassador that Mary accepted the marriage because she thought Elizabeth wanted her to wed an Englishman and this would help her be released.[48] Not loving the Duke made no difference to marrying him, she simply thought it made sense, whereas she had nothing to gain from the action of the Catholics of the north aiming to reverse the Protestant Reformation by armed rebellion.

What the rebels were planning was treasonable so kept so secretive. To this day it is surrounded by mystery. It is clear Mary at this stage of her career had no interest in a Catholic rebellion, though she was caught up in this against her will. Antonia Fraser wrote that "she did not believe that it would do her cause any good, since the moment was hardly ripe for such a demonstration", but she also wrote "Leslie later testified that she had asked him to try and get Northumberland to stop or stay the rising".[49] Leslie wrote to the Earl as he was a Percy, the dominant family in the North, though the Earl of Westmorland was more militant under pressure from his wife - and the major pressure came from catholic gentry. Mary was not pushing for rebellion and Elizabeth's later claim that Mary was "the principal cause of these troubles" has no foundation in fact. But what Mary thought was irrelevant. She was involved though locked away with her focus on her marriage hopes.

Even if Mary did not approve, a connection between her marriage plan and the rebellion is often assumed. For example, P J Holmes[50] argued "It is agreed that the rebellion grew in some way out of a conspiracy among courtiers to arrange the marriage of Mary and the Duke of Norfolk. Mary clearly played a part in this affair... meanwhile, real plotting had been going on in the North in 1569 and there is no doubt that Mary was involved". There is no real connection. Mary knew about the plot, but asked the rebels to call it off. The rebellion did not grow out of the conspiracy to marry Mary and the Duke, and it is time to see the two plots as being separate while running on parrallel lines. The Marriage plan was the first to make waves.

Barriers to a marriage

Her proposed marriage to the Duke Mary believed was uncontroversial, but she did not understand how opposed Elizabeth would always be. Elizabeth in 1569 wanted Mary to go back to Scotland. She certainly did not want her rival married to an Englishman living in England vigorously pursuing her claim to the English throne. The politicians in the court had no illusions about Elizabeth's views - so they discussed the plan behind closed doors. The court was well aware that unauthorised marriages of women with claims on the throne produced Royal paranoia. The case of Lady Katherine Grey sounded a clear warning.

Katherine/Catherine Grey, was a sister to Lady Jane Grey, beheaded for her part in the plot to prevent Mary Tudor, Elizabeth's half sister from becoming Queen in 1554. The Grey sisters were descended from Henry VII and their claim to the throne was their downfall: Antonia Fraser commenting "in the 1560s it was

Lady Catherine who was regarded by parliament as the most likely successor to Elizabeth by the English parliament.... (As) she was protestant and English and the attempts of Katherine to marry were opposed by Elizabeth.[51] Her first marriage to Lord Pembroke's son was dissolved, presumably as not given Royal approval, and Katherine then made the serious mistake of falling in love with and marrying the Earl of Hertford in 1560 - without Royal permission. They knew this was essential given Katherine's heritage, but Elizabeth did not know Hertford was married when he was sent abroad on a Crown mission. He left with his wife pregnant. The Queen was completely unaware.

Increasingly desperate, Katherine told Robert Dudley, Elizabeth's favourite and Earl of Leicester, who had the poisoned chalice of telling the Queen about the marriage. Elizabeth was furious and sent her cousin to the Tower, followed by Hertford when he returned. The couple could not show witnesses of their marriage or the priest who carried it out, they were not believed and their children were declared illegitimate - so could not inherit the throne. The lovers were then locked in the Tower of London. The Lieutenant of the Tower being sympathetic to the young couple allowed them to meet, but when another son was born in 1563 Elizabeth was incandescent with rage. The two lovers never met again. Katherine died in 1568 at the age of 27 leaving two motherless children, a tragic victim of Elizabeth's fear of being replaced.

There is no doubt Leicester and Norfolk both knew this history, but believed dynasty cut more than one way. Powerful interests in both Scotland and England wanted a solution to Mary being in limbo and marriage to a leading English aristocrat had been seen as a way forward. James Stuart's first reaction was to support an English marriage as keeping his half sister out of Scotland, but as Protestants both he and Dudley came to realise that such a marriage with a pro-Catholic nobleman, even if nominally a Protestant, would favour the Catholics. Norfolk was plotting with powerful nobles who resented the rise of commoners with talent like Cecil and Walsingham and he had potential allies for a court rebellion - if not for overthrowing Elizabeth. However no one could predict how affairs would develop. If Elizabeth died, Mary could become English Queen, and there would then be nothing to stop a Catholic crusade under her banner to reconvert England and Scotland. Leicester told the Queen what was being planned and she confronted the Duke "commanding him to free himselfe of it, for the fidelity and loyalty sake which he ought to beare unto his sovereign" and from late summer 1569 Norfolk was shunned at court as everyone knew the Queen had banned the marriage. Her paranoia over the plan forced Norfolk into a corner.

The marriage was not part of the discussions in the North, and the court knew little of the Northern rebels, believing the threat came from Norfolk releasing Mary from imprisonment in Derbyshire by armed force. Norfolk did appear to be on the verge of rebellion- and there was no standing army to stop him marching a peasant army into the Midlands to seize his intended bride.

On 15th September Norfolk angered by his marriage being banned left the court without permission, to go back to Norfolk where he had feudal control over his tenants and they would obey orders to march and fight for him. The court feared he had gone back to his estates to raise an army of revolt and on September 21st Mary was moved back to Tutbury for a second time from Derbyshire in case the Duke marched armed tenants from his estates north to force a marriage.[52] Both properties were north of the Trent, but Tutbury was fortified where Wingfield was not and a fort was now needed.

J B Black suggests that "Strictly speaking, the rebellion should have begun when Norfolk, disappointed of his purpose, left the court in high dudgeon in September, and betook himself to his country house (in Norfolk TF) at Kenninghall. ....But the Duke was a coward".[53]

Whether he was a coward or not, on September 24th he wrote to the Queen a submissive letter and was ordered back to court. Norfolk was not going to rebel and he had few links with the rebels of the north who were preparing for an armed uprising, probably when the harvest was gathered in and they could hope to mobilise the tenants on their own estates. Norfolk sent a message to his brother in law, Westmoreland, asking the rebellion to be abandoned as he could be executed if they marched. The two earls with Lord Dacre had agreed to rise on October 7th but when they received the letter decided not to rebel. Leonard Dacre went to London for a court hearing and it appeared the rebellion would be postponed. On October 2nd Norfolk was put under house arrest in London, and when the news reached the Rebels in the North this put the rebellion back on track.

By October 8th Norfolk was locked in the Tower suspected of treason. When news Norfolk was in the Tower reached the north country the rebel plotters reacted, Northumberland and Westmorland fearing they were likely to be arrested as well. Calls to go to the Privy Council were ignored, similar calls to go to York to be interrogated by the Earl of Sussex, Lord President of the Council of the North, were evaded and on November 9th Northumberland and Westmorland having decided to go to York would mean their arrest, told their supporters that the long discussed Catholic rebellion was happening. The aim was never to secure Norfolk's marriage with Mary Stuart - the northern Rebels had only ever calculated whether they could mobilise Catholics against the crown

The rebels in the north and the exile in Tutbury

Mary in Tutbury had very little influence over what was happening. The Northern Earls never said they were in touch - they could not make a statement that they wanted Mary as the rallying point for fear of putting Mary in danger - and Fraser created a muddle which lasts to this day by saying the rebellion was not much to do with her, arguing "This rising, ill prepared and ill organised, was more in the nature of a separatist movement on behalf of northern catholics than a revolt on behalf of Mary Queen of Scots".[54]

However the broad objectives were ones that profoundly affected Mary even if she did not personally see armed uprising as a good move in 1569. The rebels were Catholics intending to overthrow the protestant government in London, reverse the Reformation, make Elizabeth a puppet queen, and release Mary. If removing Cecil and other protestant ministers was not enough to control the government then Mary Stuart could provide an alternative head of state - but this could never be stated because of the threat of violence to her while imprisoned. However the fact that Mary was in the country made a profound difference compared with the anti reformation uprisings Henry VIII faced- the Pilgrimage of Grace of 1536 and other risings, the Pilgrimage alone having attracted some 40,000 rebels.

It had involved Sir Thomas Percy, the father of the Earl of Northumberland who was eight years old when his father was executed for treason on 2nd June 1537. In 1569 the Earl remembered his father's death and why the Catholics had failed against Henry VIII. Then the Catholics had no figurehead of the stature of an annointed queen which Mary would provide, and while the leaders had nothing to gain by saying they would march on Tutbury to release Mary, this was what the government had to expect. Wingfield was a large mansion but was not fortified, so the first move when the government had nothing to go on but suspicion was to move her south to Tutbury.

Mary was moved to Tutbury on September 21st and the garrison then had to assume that an attack was being planned to release her. Shrewsbury as the Queen's Jailer knew the Castle needed more troops to defeat the attack of an army so he enlisted help from the Earl of Huntingdon - at Ashby de la Zouch - and Viscount Hereford - at Chartley - to supply extra soldiers but they had only a few hundred. The Crown had no standing army to send when facing a major crisis. The background to what happened at Tutbury was fear that rebels were on the way. In the uncertainty about what was happening the government had issues with Shrewsbury's ability to cope in an armed conflict and these came to a head when Mary arrived at Tutbury for the second time.

Changes were made at Tutbury, officially because Shrewsbury was ill. On 22nd September Elizabeth wrote to the Earl of Huntingdon a very strange letter which appointed him as jailer for Mary queen of Scots in a very back handed way, telling him he would "take charge of the custody of her.... this direction of you may seame presently sodayne and strange, for you to take charge of her in any other person's house than in your owne...." but Huntingdon was forbidden to take her to Leicestershire where he had his main base. He was to keep Mary in Tutbury and not take her to his own castle at Ashby de la Zouch a dozen miles away in Leicestershire, and he was given clear instructions to work with Shrewsbury to reduce Mary's party to the accepted number of 30 and that she should not " have such liberty to send postes as she hath done...".[55]

Mary wrote to the French ambassador in London, La Mothe Fenelon, "Si je demeure un temps ici, je ne perdrai seulement mon royaume mais la vie" - "If I live here for a time I will lose not just my royalty but my life".[56] The threat was clearly the presence of a known enemy at Tutbury. And that enemy was the Earl of Huntingdon.

Henry Hastings, third Earl of Huntingdon, caused turmoil in the Privy Council. Huntingdon while very well connected - he was married to Robert Dudley's sister - was not trusted by Elizabeth as he had a strong claim to the throne via Plantagenet ancestors- both his grandmothers were descended from the Plantagenets. Indeed this was one area where both queens agreed, as Mary feared Huntingdon would have her poisoned to remove her from the line of succession and Mary's complaint he was a threat to her, was one Elizabeth was prepared to listen to - she was always alert to the threat of a near relation. Mary was making her views known, and the atmosphere at Tutbury could only have been deeply toxic.

In the Castle the two Earls, Shrewsbury and Huntingdon, awaited orders. On 28th October Cecil wrote another strange letter to Huntingdon, trying to explain a debate that day in Privy Council on whether he or Sir Ambrose Cave should replace Shrewsbury, saying "wherein no mistrust was made of yow but to excuse the challenge which the Q(ueen) of Scots maketh to yow"[57] and he was appointed on a temporary basis. - neither Queen trusted Huntingdon - then the Earl was taken out of the position on November 18th though the Northern Rebellion was alight and a rebel army was marching south. Shrewsbury had the safe pair of hands in the crisis now developing.

The rebels take up arms

The North had never accepted the protestant reformation despite the defeat of the Pilgramage of Grace and other rebellions against Henry VIII. The three Northern noblemen who had for months been plotting a catholic rebellion- the Earls of Northumberland and Westmorland and Lord Dacre - had considerable support in a region still inclined to the Catholic religion. While Mary was at Bolton Castle plans had been made to seize the Scottish Regent, her half brother the Earl of Moray when he travelled through the region on his way back to Scotland after the Casket Letters inquiry, to allow her to become Scottish Queen again. In January 1569 when they learned she was being moved to Tutbury the plotters had offered to intercept the convoy and set her free. Mary refused both offers. She wanted to regain the Scottish throne with English support not take part in a rebellion against Queen Elizabeth.

In 1568 and 1569 exile seemed to Mary to be the prelude to Elizabeth supporting her with arms, a rebellion against the Crown was not part of her script. Marriage to Norfolk was her priority, and though Norfolk was brother in law to Westmorland the Duke as a southerner was not part of the Northern plot. The rebellion which was brewing was not about the marriage, but was about the Catholic religion. The rebels wanted Mary on board, but their commitment to Norfolk was marginal

The key plotter, the Earl of Northumberland, Thomas Percy, was the greatest Lord in the region and when Darnley, a catholic, had married Mary, also a Catholic, a key Catholic activist, Richard Norton went to Northumberland to offer 700 of his own tenants and the Scots for a joint rising against Elizabeth.[58] Northumberland had refused to rebel against Elizabeth, being reluctant as his own father, also Thomas Percy and the second son of the 5th Earl, had been executed for his part in the follow up to the Pilgrimage of Grace, Bigod's rebellion of 1537. But as the 7th Earl, he resented the way his religion and feudal power was attacked by Elizabeth's government, and listened to talk of rebellion especially when Westmorland and Dacre were part of the discussion.

By the autumn the rebels decided to rise, not to back Norfolk but because after he was locked in the Tower they feared their turn was next. The northern leaders were not friendly to Norfolk though they may have favoured Mary as their figurehead, but only if they could capture her and turn her into a Catholic rallying point: but this they could not say for putting her life at risk. After the rebellion had started the two earls issued three statements, none of which mentioned Mary by name. The first was purely about religion. In a detailed study K J Kesselring quotes the statement crucially that

"Diverse, disordered, and ill disposed persons about the Queen's majesty have.... overthrown in this realm the true and catholic religion.... and now lastly seeketh to procure the destruction of the nobility. We therefore have gathered ourselves together to resist force by force..."[59]

and in a second proclamation again stressed the religious nature but added that foreign powers were likely to invade and the English should act before they arrived -perhaps promises of foreign aid had been made - arguing if they did not rebel "and foreigners enter into us we should be all made slaves and bondsmen to them".[60] Apart from the threat of slavery this suggested a foreign invasion had been flagged up - a prospect which tied the rebellion into international politics with the expectation of foreign intervention.which may have been the fall back position if they could not seize Mary.*

A third proclamation did make reference to the Succession of the Crown, but without mentioning Mary Stuart, but having an odd sentence directed at "all manner of persons to whom of mere right the true succession of the Crown appertaineth, dangerously and uncertainly depending by reason of many title and interest pretended to the same".[61] Whether this was aimed at Mary in her prisons after she had dragged her feet in backing the rebellion is impossible to say. Records of when Mary's party had been in touch with the rebel leaders are sketchy. In this third statement the names of Norfolk, and the Earls of Arundel and Pembroke were added. They immediately denied any involvement, but by this point the rebels were on the march. Kesselring reports they saw themselves as a religious army. "the men carried flags with the emblems of saints. They marched under time-hallowed banners that depicted the five wounds of Christ... one informant later... (said) they had openly worn "the ensign order of these rebels": great crucifixes about the neck".[62]

On November 14th the Earls led armed men into Durham Cathedral, celebrated the illegal Catholic Mass, and mobilised thousands to march south. When the news reached Tutbury, Shrewsbury wrote to London that he had put another 100 guards on the Castle, posted mounted scouts and ordered a search for weapons six miles around. Shrewsbury may have heard that a rapid raid by men on horseback was planned to overwhelm the defences and release the Queen, his actions show he was firmly in charge. Black states that Lord Hunsdon marching north to fight the rebels reported to London he heard from loyalists guarding the River

Don that the rebel target was to release Mary from Tutbury.[63] The government had to expect that an attack on Tutbury was planned.

Tutbury was not secure against an army - the rebels had around 6000 men - and on 22nd November the government sent orders to move Mary south of the Trent. She was moved out of Tutbury via Huntingdon's castle at Ashby de la Zouch arriving in Coventry on 25th November. The only place of imprisonment was an inn, the castle like Chartley being ruined, and Shrewsbury found the local people treating Mary as celebrity- tall, beautiful and sparkled with the stardust of royalty, her very presence was causing a commotion. Four hundred troops were put around the inn to stop the local people seeing her.[64] This was the decisive moment in the failure of the rebellion. The rebels had reached Branham Moor, south of the River Wharfe, on November 22nd, with 3800 foot soldiers and 1600 horsemen, stayed two days and then retreated northward.[65] They occupied Hartlepool, presumably waiting for a promised invasion force that never arrived. Elizabeth's armies outnumbered them and they were routed in only a few weeks. Mary heard the news in Coventry and made no recorded comment.

She stayed there over Christmas. It is said some 900 footsoldiers in the rebel army were hung, their bodies left to rot as a warning. Those of the wealthier rebels who were not hung, drawn and quartered as traitors were driven to penury by punitive fines. Though foreign Catholics did not seem to get the point, English Catholicism had been terrorised into submission.

Thus ended the last Catholic rebellion, and the decisive factor was that the Scottish Queen remained firmly in the hands of Elizabeth's government. The rebels have been dismissed despite the possibility Catholicism could have had its Joan of Arc and English history would have been transformed if they had been led by an annointed Queen.

The overriding unanswered question from the Northern rebellion is whether the rebels intended to seize Tutbury and release Mary

Stuart. It was a risky strategy, and conventional historians largely dismiss it as a non-issue, along with the Rebellion as a whole. However it is likely that the prospects were investigated and played a part in rebel planning. No attempt to reach Tutbury was made though the rebels might have done so if Mary had not been moved south of the Trent to Coventry.

As it was, on January 2nd 1570 Mary was moved back to Tutbury for a third time with the rebellion contained and on the way to defeat. As the previous winter, she hated the place and its cold and damp affected her health. Shrewsbury arranged to move her to healthier accomodation and it would be a decade and a half before she returned to the county for the final decisive act of her constant attempts to become a Queen again. Her three first visits to Tutbury had taken place against a background of Catholic discontent. Open rebellion would never happen again. But the threat she posed to Elizabeth's throne would grow.

One of the main leaders later interrogated - the Earl of Northumberland - said the intention was not to put Mary on the English throne (Roberts 1975 p193) but he was never going to put Mary in danger., Some Spanish thought the plots threatened her life and should leave her out of the uprising. (OUP pp 133-4). Norfolk himself wrote to the Earls in similar vein, pleading for no revolt as it could threaten his life and that Mary should be left alone as too well guarded to be released.

Chapter 6

1570 - Plotting Escalates

In the late spring of 1570 Shrewsbury moved Queen Mary to Chatsworth and later to other properties in the north midlands. The government concluded no armed assault could happen now the Northern Revolt had been defeated, so Tutbury was not needed. As the earl had to treat Mary as a Queen in Exile, she had to have some creature comforts and companionship. Shrewsbury's wife Bess of Hardwick shared a love of embroidery with Mary Stuart - but would not travel to Tutbury to work with the Queen so Mary was moved to their houses to be confined. She left Staffordshire and did not return till 1585.

These years were the years when she abandoned hopes that Elizabeth 1 would put her back on the Scottish throne, putting her energies into plots to seize the positions she craved through foreign support, with the English Catholics only having a role if they had foreign backing. In the summer of 1570 she preferred support from Elizabeth to plans for revolution.

This was her position once a local plot in Chatsworth in summer 1570 failed to provide any plans to get her out of the country. Mary's Master of household John Beaton still hoped that Elizabeth would put her back on the Scottish throne, and told the plotters "she nothing doubted but that the Queen's Majesty (Elizabeth)... would restore her to her former dignity hereafter the which (sic) she rather minded to expect, than to adventure on a mere uncertainty...".[66] But failure turned her towards violent catholic uprising. P J Holmes commented the plot involved "the assassination of Elizabeth,...

release Mary from captivity and if possible arrange a foreign invasion at the same time. This was a trick which no one even came close to pulling off".[67] But this came to be Mary's favoured plan and was to run through to the Babbington plot, which brought her to the block. The scheme looked feasible and took in the Duke of Norfolk who became involved in the Ridolfi plot as 1570 turned to 1571.

Ridolfi - plotter with Mary and the Duke

As Mary Stuart had not helped plan the Earls Rebellion, and Norfolk had surrendered to the crown and was locked in the Tower of London during the conflict. They could not be accused of treasonable activity during the Northern revolt and avoided the trials and executions which followed. Mary was moved out of Tutbury and Norfolk released from the Tower. By the summer of 1570 they appeared to have weathered the storm. Mary naively believed that Elizabeth would allow the marriage, and Fraser comments that in January 1570 she wrote to Norfolk that "'I believe the Queen of England and country should like it"...When she had had considerable evidence to the contrary'".[68] As 1570 showed she was chasing after a shadow, she came to realise this was futile and responded to Catholic excommunication of Elizabeth 1 by embracing conspiracy..

The Pope reacted to the brutal suppression of the Northern revolt by excommunicating Elizabeth in February 1570 releasing Catholics from any duty to obey the Elizabethan Protestant government. While most Catholics ignored the papal bull a militant minority did not. However while domestic rebellion had to be backed by foreign invasion, it was equally clear no invasion could succeed unless Mary was safely released. Norfolk now worked on plots to do this. He now had a reputation as a coward and the execution of Northumberland plus the exile of his brother in law Westmorland and Northumberland's cousin Leonard Dacre reinforced this. To redeem himself Norfolk went back into plotting on behalf of the Catholic church. When he was released from the Tower in the summer he chose to work with Roberto Ridolfi, who he had contacted before the Northern rebellion.

Ridolfi, an Italian banker based in London, was an agent of the Pope intent reversing the Reformation. He aimed to put Mary on the English - and Scottish - thrones through a Catholic uprising backed by a foreign invasion. The Spanish Ambassador in London, Don Guerau de Spes reported to Madrid that on February 29th 1568 Ridolfi had approached him on behalf of Norfolk and Lords Lumley and Arundel to secure support for a revolution to remove William Cecil and bring back Catholicism. Nothing came of this, as the Spanish commander in the Netherlands, the Duke of Alva (or Alba), saw this as impossible without more naval and military resources, which the Spanish King did not have. Perhaps promises were made , but no military aid came to Hartlepool in 1569, a port secured by the northern rebels possibly to take an invasion fleet.

The Italian had been a channel for money from the Pope to reach the Northern rebels and other Catholic players - at the height of the northern revolt on 22nd November 1569 the Bishop of Ross (Mary Stuart's London Ambassador) received £2916 paid by Ridolfi on behalf of de Spes for Mary's use.[69] Ridolfi was trusted by the Papacy, Mary and Phillip II of Spain - but Alva saw Ridolfi's intrigues as unworkable. Alva would have been even more sceptical had he known that on the eve of the Northern revolt Ridolfi had been arrested by Francis Walsingham, whose main job at this time was as a diplomat - he was Ambassador to France till 1573, when he returned home to be a Privy Councillor - but was now working with William Cecil as a brilliant if ad hoc counter espionage chief.

Ridolfi had not been put in the Tower but in Walsingham's house under house arrest. Ridolfi made a deal - exchanging information for his freedom, probably supplying Walsingham with the codes used by de Spes to write to Norfolk and Alva. Ridolfi supplying the codes would enable Walsingham, not for the last time, to read subversive correspondence. Before the Northern revolt Ridolfi had been approached by Norfolk and Lord Lumley to talk about an anti -Cecil alliance, but he was playing a double cross game which Norfolk would have been well advised to avoid, the Duke was fatally seduced by the intrigue of a Catholic powerplay.

In 1570 once Mary moved out of Tutbury and Norfolk was released from the Tower plotting recommenced using Norfolk as the main player - Mary was of course locked away relying on coded letters to make sense of what was going on. Norfolk had been released from the Tower and though was not allowed to go back to his feudal estate - he would never see his house at Kenninghall again - he had made a robust defence of his innocence of any role in the Northern Rebellion in December. The main development in late 1570 was that Elizabeth's ministers devised new plans for Mary to return to Scotland, Cecil and Sir Walter Mildmay, the protestant Chancellor of the Exchequer, visited her in Chatsworth and started three way talks, the Scots being involved. In March 1571 the Scots said any more talks would need a meeting of the Scots parliament, and on March 23rd Elizabeth called a halt till this was held. As the spring came on, the negotations, which tried Mary's patience, were put in the shade by the slow discovery of the Ridolfi plot.

By September 1570 Ridolfi sent the Pope a new plan allegedly devised by Norfolk and other anti Cecil Peers to "free Mary and restore religion".[70] Norfolk was tempted by the reward of becoming joint ruler of the new Catholic state after marrying Mary. Mary could not have been directly involved in planning, but sent correspondence in support of the plan.

Ridolfi went to Rome in March 1571 via his home town of Florence, where he told Cosimo de Medici the Grand Duke of Tuscany of the plot. The Duke, Catherine de Medici's brother, shared his sisters' dislike of the Guise family - Mary's mother was a Guise - and sent the plan to London, Ridolfi had no idea the politics of Tuscany might lead to the plan going straight to Elizabeth 1, confirming Alva's view the man was a windbag. Phillip of Spain never lost faith in Ridolfi and was obsessed with The Enterprise of England as the plotters called it. Cecil, now Lord Burghley had the outline by mid April.[71] But the outline did not specify details as Spain had not agreed to back Ridolfi's plan at this point.

The plan involved Norfolk organising a Catholic rising, toppling Elizabeth, taking over the throne with his new wife Mary, with Spain sending an invasion force which Philip II imagined would be so well supported by the Catholics the new regime could take over both England and Scotland. The civil war which would follow was seen as a minor matter. Philip met with Ridolfi, was convinced, and sent a secret letter to Alva in the Netherlands on 14th July 1571 arguing Norfolk could easily kill Elizabeth, stating he "Has the resolve and so many and such prominent friends that if I provide some help it would be easy for him to kill or capture Elizabeth and to place the Scottish Queen at liberty and in possession of the throne".[72] Did he not realise Norfolk was being closely watched?

Alva, who would have to provide 'some help' in the form of a seaborne invasion, was horrified - he was a blunt soldier who knew it was easy to start a fight but harder to win it, and had little faith Norfolk had the military experience required. He wrote back to his King arguing "Your Majesty says that it is not your intention to take a course of action that would lead to the outbreak of war with our neighbours, and elsewhere Your Majesty tells me that you wish to help the Duke of Norfolk.... which, done in the way you describe, is a clear and direct declaration of war.".[73] Alva feared the English going to war to support the protestant rebels in the Netherlands and tying down his army. Phillip had however become enamoured with his plot and believed Mary and the Duke of Norfolk were blessed by God, this being enough to make a deadly conspiracy work perfectly. Philip wrote that once Mary and Norfolk were married they would "without difficulty reduce England to the obedience of the Holy See". Despite the King's naivety, however, what emerged was a serious plan to overthrow the English government involving Mary Stuart.

Elizabeth's spies could not penetrate the Spanish regime but news of the plot came through over the course of 1571 anyway. Cosimo di Medici sent the outline from Florence. When the protestant Scottish army captured Dumbarton Castle from Catholics on the night of April 2-3 they found evidence of Mary communicating with Alva and sent the correspondence to Cecil. The Queen of Navarre sent Elizabeth evidence of the plot against her from a Spanish courier intercepted in the Pyrenees. In May one Charles Bailly was intercepted at Dover with books and letters intended for John Leslie, Bishop of Ross and chief advisor to Mary Stuart. The code names on the letters - 'Trente' and 'Quarante' were not immediately identified, but proved to be Norfolk and Lord Lumley on later investigation.[74]

Fraser says "the connection of Leslie and Ridolfi was a fatal one for Mary, because Leslie led directly to the Scottish Queen, whose envoy he was"[75] but even more damaging were the links discovered with Norfolk. If 'Trente' was unknown at first, it was easy to make the connection when Higford, Norfolk's secretary, and his agents Barker and Bannister, were discovered trying to send money to support the Scottish Catholics who still at that point had armed forces and could be capable of restoring the Queen- they were losing key fortifications like Dumbarton but were still a major threat in 1571. The money did not get to them and both Black in the Oxford history and Fraser suggests that it was this discovery which brought Mary to be investigated

The Spanish connection was alarming and the fact Mary was writing to Alva worried government ministers, but they had a lack of evidence against her or Norfolk on a charge of conspiring with a foreign power. Early September brought a breakthrough.

Though Spain was the superpower of sixteenth century Europe a major problem which prevented the country launching an Armada was lack of sufficient sea going ships. Two English mercenary sea captains, George Fitzwilliam and John Hawkins, well known for fighting the Spanish navy in the Carribean, and seen as guns for hire in Madrid, had agreed to provide additional boats. But these were double agents and Fitzwilliam returned from Spain with full details of the planned invasion, arriving on September 4th, telling Hawkins and then Cecil. The Secretary of State immediately took action, on 5th September 1571 sending a top priority letter to Shrewsbury -marked HASTE, HASTE, POST HASTE FOR LIFE, LIFE, LIFE ordering Mary to be close confined to prevent her escaping to Spain and to interrogate her about her "labour's and devices to stir up a new rebellion in this realm and to have the King of Spain assist it"Cecil noting that "she made choise to go into Spayne than to Scotland or France".[76] Elizabeth had not been concerned about her plans for gaining her freedom, nor offering her son to a Spanish marriage or even having plans for marrying Don Juan of Austria, but inciting a rebellion with a Spanish invasion in support was a direct threat to her personally.

Cecil demanded the Earl "shall do well to send the names of those that shall remayne and of such as shall depart" so the government could keep track of who was seeing the exile: but it does not appear that she was to be forbidden to have visitors. Unlike Norfolk, she was still treated with kid gloves.

Norfolk was arrested and sent to the Tower on September 7th 1571. He would now be put on trial for treason. There had been much known to the government about the Ridolfi plot, but information on the planned invasion from Spanish sources had been missing until Fitzwilliam supplied it. Mary was seen as an international player, this clarifying English priorities: the enemy was now Spain. Hawkins would be appointed treasure of the navy in 1578 [77] - An Armada was to be expected so the navy had to be modernised - Hawkins and his colleagues were the ideal people to modernise the English navy - having fought in the Spanish Main they knew how to build better ships. This lay in the future, but it was now clear to English protestants by 1571-72, Mary Stuart was the centre of the storms that were coming towards them- along with the Duke of Norfolk.

Elizabeth versus parliament

Hard evidence Norfolk had been working in the interests of a foreign power now existed. He would be accused of working for an invasion by Spanish forces, and supporting Scottish catholic rebels, his secretary seeking to send gold coin to Mary's supporters in Scotland proving decisive. Mary had sent at least one coded letter of support which was cited in the trial. Norfolk faced interrogation on a charge of undermining both states and his defence was unconvincing. He was convicted of High Treason for his role in the plot. The Scots were friendly and Norfolk was undoubtedly guilty of High Treason - and this was a capital offence - but Elizabeth was reluctant to act, twice cancelling the death warrant. Parliament, which had removed Catholics after the excommunication of Elizabeth, was furious and feelings began running high.

MPs demanded that Mary be put on trial, assuming she would be found guilty and executed. Mary's correspondence with Norfolk apparently supporting the Ridolfi plot and cited at his trial became an issue. The Commons and Lords in committee agreed she should be attainted and charged with treason. The convocation of senior clergy reached the same conclusion. The Bardon Papers sum up parliamentary attitudes of a body which saw Mary Stuart as the hostile ally of a foreign power.[78] The petition on removing Mary Stuart from the succession to the throne was not a petition as we would know it, signed by supporters, but is a 15 page document on the reasons for blocking her path to the throne. It is highly significant, but less significant than the response of Elizabeth 1. She refused to take any action.

Lords and Commons proposed a Bill which would take away Mary's claim to the throne. Elizabeth refused to allow it to be passed, using the evasive formula *la royne s'advisera*- the Queen will think (take advice) on it. She may or may not have taken counsel - if so, it did not include her closest advisor, William Cecil who wrote to Walsingham in France that he had been thwarted, complaining that "All that we have laboured for, and had with full consent brought to fashion - I mean a law to make the Scottish Queen unable and unworthy of succession to the crown - was by Her Majesty neither assented to nor rejected, but deferred".[79]

Cecil and Walsingham came to the conclusion that Elizabeth would not only refuse to exclude Mary from the throne, but would block attempts to prevent her plotting Regicide. Shrewsbury was allowed to continue the lax regime in his houses - Mary not only took the waters at Buxton in Derbyshire but Shrewsbury built her a secure house for the purpose, possibly starting the destruction of his marriage to Bess of Hardwick by so doing as he seemed unduly sympathetic to Mary. He knew Mary might become Queen - while the militant anti Marians among the ministers realised after 1572 they were trapped in a vicious Catch 22. Elizabeth would only act against Mary if presented with undeniable evidence that her cousin had backed her murder. It had to be assumed that Mary was not stupid enough to write that this was her policy -and this was the only evidence Elizabeth would accept.

But Elizabeth could not defend Norfolk, who had been convicted of treason as an increasingly belligerent parliament pointed out. Norfolk would have to be sacrificed to ward off the clamour against Mary. Elizabeth always suffered in authorising executions when the person was known to her. Faced with the conviction of Norfolk, she had an emotional breakdown in March 1572 so severe Cecil and Leicester - the advisors so dear to her she gave them nicknames - spent three nights at her bedside. Eventually she recovered and gave the order. Norfolk was executed on 2nd June 1572 a month before parliament ended. Mary was distraught. Another partner had suffered violent death largely because of knowing her.

Shrewsbury was under pressure from ministers to tighten the hold over Mary, but admitted himself he could not control her letter writing and plotting. In March 1575 he told an anxious William Cecil "What intellygens passeth for this Quene to and fro my house I doo not know".[80] Given that Mary ceaselessly sought ways to become Queen and the Ridolfi plot had led to the execution of her intended husband, Cecil would not have found this good news.

Mary was now untouchable unless she signed a written statement sanctioning Elizabeth's murder. A dozen years would pass without any change to the policy of Elizabeth turning a blind eye to her cousin's plotting. There was no doubt she would continue to seek power by gambling with dangerous conspiracies. Her brother in law, no political genius, was able to see that this could have only one outcome. Watching events from France, Charles IX said "The poor fool will never cease (from plotting JW) until she loses her head. In faith, they will put her to death. I see it is her own fault and folly".[81]

This prediction would come true, but remarkably, with Shrewsbury and others following Elizabeth's lead to treat her with kid gloves, the protestant belief she posed a mortal threat had no impact.. For a decade, Mary continued to plan ways to be Queen of two countries, living a charmed life confined in luxurious houses provided by Shrewsbury and his wife. Bess of Hardwick. She was in a cul de sac politically, aiming to break back into a world of power she had been educated to expect as her birthright, but with her supporters unable to find ways to bring about the end of her confinement, while her opponents were unable to bring an end to her plotting.

Chapter 7

1572-1584 The gathering storm

Between 1572 and 1584 Mary Stuart's life entered a limbo without the high profile crises which gave her life drama, a period of relative calm which is however easily misunderstood . For example, Jenny Wormald commented "at the end of 1571, after the discovery of the Ridolfi plot, Elizabeth allowed ... the Casket letters to be published. The following decade saw something of a lull. Mary lived mainly in Sheffield Castle, though occasionally spending periods elsewhere, at Tutbury and Chartley".[82] There was indeed a lull, but the Queen did not live in Staffordshire between summer 1570 and the end of 1584. The isolation of the Staffordshire countryside only happened when crisis demanded she be put in lockdown- and these did not occur till 1585, so for nearly a decade and a half Shrewsbury could handle her with kid gloves. Perhaps suprisingly, this was the tacit policy of Elizabeth 1.

The Ridolfi plot had led to a storm around Mary's head, but she survived intact because Elizabeth protected her apparently assuming she would behave herself - she was next in line to the throne and for Elizabeth that was crucial. There was an invisible protective cordon around her, erected by the English Queen, blocking the opposition of ministers like Cecil and Walsingham who could not understand this tolerance. Elizabeth's decision that plotting against her required no action allowed her cousin to live a charmed life.

The period after she left Tutbury for the third time at the end of May 1570 saw Shrewsbury keep Mary Stuart in relatively comfortable house arrest. Keeping Mary locked up was his main task which he carried out effectively, but he could not stop Mary corresponding and thus plotting. As Fraser comments, this may have been because George Talbot had very good reason to be sympathetic to his prisoner. Politicians were painfully aware the whole regime depended on the beating of Queen Elizabeth's heart. If Elizabeth died, Mary became Queen in her place. Both Protestants and Catholics took their cue from this very basic fact. Kid gloves were inevitable in dealing with the exile, allowing Catholics to plot.

Antonia Fraser wrote perceptively, "if Elizabeth died suddenly, who knew but that Mary's fortunes might not be dramatically reversed?.... This consideration of Mary's potential as queen of England, which died away in the 1580s after James grew to manhood, was very much present in the minds of the English statesmen in the 1570s...".[83] Thus in the relatively peaceful 1570s "the minor pains or pleasures of her prison routine became temporarily more important than European or Scottish politics" and "The actual conditions of her captivity were not in themselves particularly rigorous during the 1570s, except during moments of national crisis".[84] Shrewsbury was very far from taking the chance of annoying a possible Queen, a fact which also applies to her next jailer Sir Ralph Sadler for similar reasons, but does not apply after the summer of 1584, and the murder of the Dutch protestant leader, William of Orange.

But before then Shrewsbury allowed her some privileges, allowing visits to Buxton to take the waters for her health, in 1573, 1574, 1575, 1576, 1580, and 1584 - the last visit a month after the Dutch murder. The secure house built for her was intended to isolate her from the gentry who flocked there, but as Shrewsbury was known to display the Queen to visitors to boost his reputation, it is likely she did meet other visitors. The Earl was never seen as the most effective jailer. However the visits to Buxton were approved by Queen and government, and Guy comments "as far as possible (she) was kept in isolation. She did sometimes get the opportunity to speak to the other bathers".[85]

The regime in her household under Shrewsbury was only loosely supervised, and indeed all the Queen's guardians including the last, Paulet, allowed her freedom within her private quarters. It would not be until her arrest at Tixall that Elizabeth's agents entered and searched her quarters. Till then she was allowed to control her own space to the extent that her jewels were stolen from Sheffield Park in 1577 because of the laxity or dishonesty of her treasurer, a man called Dolin.[86] Even more suprisingly, Mary was always able to call on the services of a Catholic Priest. Fraser talks of two "secret priests" a Sir John Mortoun who died in her service and was succeded by another called de Preau, while in 1571 she employed a secretary - really a father confessor - one Ninian Winzet. She actually was visited by a Jesuit priest, Samerie, three times in the 1580s.[87]

Given that the Jesuits were the shock troops of the Counter Reformation, it is not suprising Shrewsbury for all his wealth and devotion to duty lost credibility as the political climate darkened in the 1580s. By August 1584 - a month after the final trip to Buxton - Sir Ralph Sadler replaced the Earl in charge of Mary Stuart, then at Sheffield and shortly to move south to Tutbury via Wingfield.

The reasons Shrewsbury was not able to carry on his role as Mary's jailer are sometime put down to his marital troubles. Kate Williams suggests gossip was spreading damagingly, commenting "Talbot had long been accused of being too kind to Mary, pushing for her to visit Buxton, allowing her huge retinue, subsidising her expenses and letting her socialise with local families. Now, everyone said, they knew why. Like so many men before him, he had been seduced by the Scots Queen".[88] There was certainly gossip, though Buxton had been approved by ministers and Shrewsbury had no choice on financial matters since Elizabeth failed to pay him the money due for keeping Mary, and it is true that. scandalous allegations were made about Mary's relationship with the Earl, but affairs of state overshadowed affairs of the heart. England was about to go to war with Catholic Spain, so government ministers felt Shrewsbury despite coping with the crisis in 1569 was too lenient to continue in charge.

From Cold War to Hot War

Elizabeth had kept England out of wars for a quarter century, but by 1583 religious conflict had intensified on both sides of the English channel. France slipped into civil war after St Bartholomew's day 1572, when Catholics massacred Protestants. The Spanish army in the Netherlands fought a bitter war against Protestant rebels, and in 1580 King Phillip of Spain put a reward on the head of William of Orange, the protestant leader. In England, an influx of priests stiffened Catholic morale especially when the Jesuits made their appearance. Some Catholics debated whether assassination was morally right. For the activists, the debate was academic and religious killings were acceptable, but Mary was careful never to go as far as approving killing Elizabeth. She was horrified - according to Antonia Fraser - at terrorist attempts to kill her cousin, but these attempts took place.

In 1581 and 1583 the lone assassins Tyrrell and Somerville attempted to kill Elizabeth, and were captured in the nick of time. Lone assassins trying to have her cousin killed only showed that Mary was not able to control individual activists. She was not opposed to killing Elizabeth but what she was looking for was a plan to secure her in the conflict which would follow Elizabeth's killing, release her from prison and allow her to take the throne. In 1583 the Throckmorton/Throgmorton plot showed the way she was thinking.

The plan was a revived version of the Ridolfi plot, this time co-ordinated by English Gentry in the form of the brothers but with an extensive network across the continent - closely linked to Mary's agents, Charles Paget (from a Staffordshire family, based at Beaudesert not far from Tutbury and Chartley - the county was divided on religious lines), plus Thomas Morgan and Charles Arundel - supported by the French Guise family's Catholic League. Mary was of course half Guise. In September 1583 the Spanish promised finance.[89]

In November 1583 the Throckmorton brothers were plotting for the overthrow of the government backed by a foreign army - and Francis was captured with lists of Catholics willing to back armed insurrection following the Ridolfi model - a Catholic rebellion on the 1569 model and the assassination of Elizabeth 1 followed by a French/Spanish invasion. The Throckmorton family was close to the throne - their uncle Nicholas had been Ambassador to Scotland when Mary was forced to abdicate - and the brothers acted with Mary's knowledge.[90] Francis was captured while writing a coded letter to Mary - raising questions about the ability of Shrewsbury as a jailer to check her correspondence - and had a document defending the right of Mary to be English Queen. Other documents included maps of ports suitable for an invasion, which he confessed would be organised by French Catholics under the Duke of Guise and the Catholic Holy League. Phillip II would pay half the costs.

The Spanish Ambassador Mendoza was expelled in January 1584 for his role in the Throckmorton plot. and there was no replacement. Guy notes that Mary had in November 1581 promised Robert Beale who was sent to negotiate with Mary that "she would accept Elizabeth as the lawful Queen of England and not have dealings with foreign powers or rebels. Within a few months however she was writing to Bernadino de Mendoza... Spanish ambassador in London, asking for information about new plots..." but in outline this was the same plan that Ridolfi invented and Throckmorton pursued. There is no sign that Mendoza invented the Babington conspiracy, but there is no doubt that diplomacy was not his priority and that Mary Stuart was involved in rebellion whatever promises she made.

When interrogated Throckmorton said that Mary knew all the details of the plan. She denied knowledge, but Elizabeth concluded[91] "her intention was to lull us into security, that we might less seek to discover practices at home and abroad". Yet the Queen still refused to put Mary on trial for treason. Burghley wrote a note to himself[92] "To have regard to Sheffield". Mary was kept by Shrewsbury in his properties at Sheffield and he was less and less trusted as a jailer. The fact that Mary was still technically a 'guest' and had privileges meant that her correspondence could not be tracked nor her files checked - so threats the government could not assess had no response.

Burghley and Walsingham set up the Bond Of Association, a league of Protestants pledged to defend Elizabeth threatening to pursue "by force of arms as by all other means of revenge" anyone putting the Queen at risk. But when Parliament considered an "Act for the Queen's safety" this was modified on Elizabeth's orders to avoid threatening James Stuart, who was safely protestant, and posed no threat to the English system of government. This was not the case with his mother, but Elizabeth would not approve of mob law and in March 1585 Elizabeth signed the Bill into law only when a clause setting up a tribunal to try anyone who would benefit from her death was added.[93] She insisted on legality as she did not want her cousin murdered.. Mary was shown the bond on the 5th January 1585 and promptly offered to sign it. This was a futile gesture which did not stop her being moved back to Tutbury a fourth time nine days later. She was the perceived threat whatever she did. Still worse, continental politicians did not trust her agents, notably Morgan and Paget, with the invasion plans as they were playing political games which undermined the overall plan. The Jesuit Samerie warned Mary personally that Morgan and Paget were unreliable: the Parry case underlined the dangers.[94]

At the start of 1585 William Parry, a spy who was employed by the government to keep track of Catholic plots proved turncoat and was arrested when found to be approaching the Queen while armed with intent to kill. His interrogation revealed that Mary's agent in Paris, Thomas Morgan, had encouraged his effort.[95] Morgan was put in prison in France but not extradited or tried, and remained plotting from the Bastille, a clear sign of French tolerance though not clearly a sign Mary was linked to the French government. Antonia Fraser points out that at her trial Mary denied Morgan was in her pay. [96] She had written to Elizabeth condemning the attack, and to the French ambassador - and may have been genuinely shocked. What the episode showed was that Morgan was beyond her control, and she should have understood her network in France was unreliable.

But Mary's shock was in part because her own survival was threatened by random attempts to kill Elizabeth. A well executed plan with an attempt to save her before the forces of the Bond of Association could get to her was attractive to her. Above all, Mary wanted a foreign invasion as she knew the Catholics in England were too weak to challenge Elizabeth's forces. Fraser puts her thinking clearly: "Queen Mary was strongly predisposed towards any scheme that sounded as though it might have the backing of a major power, and strongly disinclined to consider any hare brained scheme which had exactly the opposite ring".[97] Government ministers had worked out this was her best option, and wanted to prevent her plotting with foreign powers, hence the return to Tutbury.

The reluctance of Elizabeth to react proactively to threats to her life is very odd. English and Scottish history in the sixteeenth century was brutal and violent, and all the Tudors faced serious threats. As a dynasty which had gained the throne on the battlefield, they were well aware of the maxim "Uneasy lies the head that wears the Crown". The response of monarchs to organised attempts to overthrow them were always met with torture and the cruel execution of hanging, drawing and quartering, invariably on men by men. Women were not involved and this may have been one reason why Mary was untouchable. But hardly enough to explain why she was allowed to organise a conspiracy. Mendoza believed the Spanish would support her, but this depended on the fortunes of war, and politicians could use spies to try to track developments. The domestic threat from Catholics was opaque but growing but hard to chart, and leniency was no longer a sensible policy.

Elizabeth's ministers knew a serious attempt to rescue Mary and prevent the Bond of Association killing her in retaliation for the murder of Elizabeth, required a local Catholic organisation capable of reaching her before the Bond - but could it be found?. Mary was only too aware how vulnerable she was, but never stopped plans which put her neck on the line. The return to Tutbury showed that in the game of cat and mouse which she played whenever she had supporters who might rescue her, the relatively benign treatment which operated from the execution of Norfolk to the Throckmorton Plot was no longer a possibility.

In this new climate, it was clear Shrewsbury was no longer the man to be Mary's jailer. Her custody was taken from him, and alternatives to his properties and position as jailer were sought. As a first step, she was moved out of Shrewsbury's power base in Sheffield and sent to Tutbuy via Wingfield with new jailers, Sir Ralph Sadler and his son in law John Somers. Sadler was a reluctant elderly career diplomat, who had admired Mary as a baby when Ambassador in Scotland, having no desire to be forced to keep the Queen confined. On the road to Wingfield 40 soldiers guarded the party, and Mary asked Somers if he feared she would escape. He admitted he did. She replied "I had rather die in this captivity than run away with shame".[98] In reality, she had nowhere to escape to. Without supporters to take her to safety, she had no future as a fugitive. And when she moved south, there were no supporter networks anywhere. Sadler was an experienced, hard nosed diplomat, not a romantic, and his continued lenient treatment - he allowed her to go hawking - was based on a realistic assessment that in every way, Mary had nowhere to go.

Part 3 - ENDGAME

Chapter 8

Return to Tutbury

Mary Stuart arrived back at Tutbury in the custody of Sir Ralph Sadler on 14th January 1585. Sadler took the exiled Queen to the castle on the hill a little short of 16 years after she first arrived at the prison she most detested. A new regime was beginning, with the objective being to place her in a prison where no communication with the outside world was possible. The plan, driven by government anxiety over the international situation blocked the hopes of hard line ministers who hoped to get Mary tried for treason by finding evidence she had written that she approved murdering Elizabeth 1. This outcome was always unlikely as Mary knew approving regicide in her secret coded letters would be a serious mistake, though she assumed these would never be discovered anyway. She underestimated Walsingham's spy network, but he knew, and she assumed, he could not be sure he saw all her letters.

In theory Mary's ambition to be English Queen could wait for Elizabeth's death - she was nine years younger, but her health was worse than Elizabeth's and the future was unknowable, so she schemed. Plotting had never been enough to trigger a trial as Elizabeth's demand for an explicit death threat against her to trigger a trial was unlikely to be met. Government priorities were now to make sure Mary could not be rescued and had to be isolated to stop her corresponding with Catholic plotters. This became vital as the lessons of the Throckmorton plot sank in.

When Francis Throckmorton's list of Catholic notables prepared to join a rebellion was brought to Elizabeth she realised that Catholic support for rebellion was not confined to the old Northern strongholds of Catholicism. The most recent assassination attempts were almost at random, and the government - which lacked a police force and security service - had no way knowing where killers might come from at any moment and Shrewsbury had already admitted he was not able to monitor Mary's plots. (see footnote 80) An attempt to free Mary and launch a civil war to overthrow Elizabeth's government was now a constant threat. Elizabeth however refused to sanction legal action against Mary despite evidence that she had known about what the Throckmorton brothers were doing.. She remained adamant that Mary had to actually call for her death before she would act, and this was Catch 22 - it appeared impossible that she would incriminate herself in a murder plot. .

The crisis which led to Mary coming back to Tutbury developed over 1584. Andrea Clarke of the British Library analysing government letters concludes that "There is a palpable sense of heightened levels of fear among Elizabeth's government and ministers about her (Elizabeth's) safety in the midst of the danger posed by Mary Queen of Scots". Mary was always the provocation and inspiration for the Catholic cause, and the government had lost confidence that the Earl of Shrewsbury could keep her from contact with rebel plotters. Mary realised the comfortable days of trips to Buxton to take the waters were over and on her last visit wrote[99]

Buxtona, quae calida celibriris nomine Lymphae
Forte mihi post hac non adeunda, Vale
(Buxton, whose warm waters have made thy name famous,
perchance I shall visit thee no more - farewell)

What happened to her depended on international developments which after the expulsion of the Spanish ambassador Mendoza in January 1584 saw diplomatic relations with Spain broken off and England slide into open warfare with Spain. On August 10th 1585

Elizabeth signed a treaty with the Dutch to send an army to fight in the Low countries against the Spanish army commanded by the Duke of Alba. Elizabeth had avoided war fearing the Catholic super powers France and Spain joining up to invade, but the threat of two power invasion dwindled when the Guise Catholic League became embroiled in Civil War in France. Emotional turmoil in Shrewsbury's household was not the reason for Mary arriving back in Tutbury.

As Phillip II had made putting Mary on the English throne a key objective since the Ridolfi plot, she was a player in the war strategy of both sides. From the early 1580s she was drawn back into plotting as the Throckmorton plot showed, so English preparations for war logically involved tighter control over Mary. Moving her and appointing Sadler her guardian was a step toward doing this but Sir Ralph Sadler, was not the ideal man for scrutinising Mary - he had dandled her on his knee when envoy to Scotland in the 1540s and as a career diplomat had well developed deference to royalty.

Sadler was as affected by Mary's famous charm offensive as Shrewsbury had been - even William Cecil had not been immune when he visited her in Chatsworth, speaking later of her "cunning and sugared entertainment of all men".[100] Sadler had allowed her to go hawking with insufficient supervision and when travelling through Derby she had spoken to several local people.[101] Given the dangers of a Catholic rescue attempt, Sadler was thought to be taking unacceptable risks. While Tutbury was well suited for close confinement, Sadler was not the ideal jailer and knew this to be so.

When Sadler was appointed on August 26th 1584 he protested he was not the right man, and wrote to Walsingham on 2nd September asking to be relieved of the duty, which the Queen agreed to on December 2nd. On 4th January 1585 Sir Amyas Paulet was appointed, but he did not take up the role till April. Sadler was merely a stop gap while someone immune to Mary's charm was found, and that person was Paulet. He did not take up his role till he had clear instructions on what was required as regime change was in the air.

Once a tougher jailer had been put in place, Elizabeth's key ministers Lord Burghley and the spy master Walsingham were in a position to move to a new proactive strategy. Diplomacy was one strand. Recognising that if Elizabeth died and Mary took over the throne there would be a civil war and if Mary won, they would be killed, they took evasive action by securing Mary's son James as the successor. It had always been the case that if Elizabeth died without naming a successor - she never did - then Mary was next in line until James reached manhood, but this was now close to being achieved - on 19th June 1585 he reached his 19th birthday and began to make serious attempts to decide his fate - in March he told his council that he would not agree to the "Association" which his mother wanted, and Antonia Fraser concludes that "James had discovered he had some of the cards, and Elizabeth had some of the others, Mary had none at all".[102]

This was re-emphasised in July 1586 when James signed the Treaty of Berwick, agreeing Scotland and England would support each other against attempts to change their religion, resist a third party invasion, and James would become a pensioner of England recieving £4000 per year. The succession was not mentioned but it was abundantly clear that James was de facto the next in line for the English throne. It was a devastating blow to his mother.[103] But unlike the protestant James, Mary was in England and if Elizabeth died suddenly and she inherited there would be severe and violent political consequences. Even if Elizabeth survived - no one knew she would live till 1603, and she had already exceeded expectations by living to be over 50 - Mary had to be contained if the government were to survive the coming Spanish invasion. Paulet was the man to contain her.

While national developments with James coming to make his own decisions in summer 1585 were crucial, what was happening in Staffordshire would bring Mary's story to its climax. Paulet like Sadler was a career diplomat but unlike Sadler was a puritan who regarded Mary as a threat to his religion and his Queen's survival and tightened security at Tutbury as he had been ordered to.

The key to stopping plotting was stopping secret letters entering and leaving. No strangers were to be allowed into the castle, walking on the walls was forbidden as it was suspected messages would be passed out, and trips out were to be supervised by armed men. Paulet's servants and Mary's must never meet, Mary's servants must not leave Tutbury, he must not admit strangers to its precincts and especially he must watch Mary's "launderesses and coachmen" to prevent clandestine correspondence being transmitted.

But there was a weakness in the plans. The launderesses lived in Tutbury town, whose houses surround the castle, and could easily hide letters in their dresses. Paulet could not strip search them, and they could take letters in and out hidden in their underclothes if they wished. Fraser points out "These elusive maidens, under the pretext of carrying on their work, had carried on a merry trade ofmessage bearing".[104]

There are few amusing facets of what happened when Paulet took over, but his perplexed comments as Robert Hutchinson reports over the challenge of "stripping them down to their smocks" (ie underclothes TF) are unintentionally funny. As Paulet commented in his letters, with so many uncouth soldiers about this "cannot be comely". The strait laced old bureaucrat was quite right. Although the stripping and searching would have been done by trusted women, the effect on military discipline would have been disasterous and Paulet could not do it. Paulet had to accept defeat where the launderesses were concerned. But while this plan may not have been workable they were not forgotten - a new solution had to be found to the problem these workers posed.[105]

Mary could not be locked away and forgotten. She certainly had to have exercise and in July 1585 Paulet allowed her to hunt deer with a greyhound, a precedent followed later - when she was fit to do so. Her health was now becoming an urgent issue. After moving to Tutbury for a fourth time, Mary could well feel she had been cornered. Antonia Fraser commented "By the spring of 1585 there was very little that was encouraging .... in the situation of the queen of Scots. Her son had repudiated her, her French organisation was in administrative chaos...Mary herself no longer felt complete trust for her erstwhile allies abroad. In the meantime her position in England may be compared to that of someone tied unwillingly over a powder keg which may at any time be exploded by a march held by an overenthusiastic friend".[106] Fraser is right that Mary was threatened by actions of people she had never heard of, so the Bond of Association supporters might attack her after violence against Elizabeth she had no idea was happening.

She could do nothing about this situation, but what was worrying the English government were signs both physically and emotionally she was deteriorating and reports to the French government, leading to protests from Paris, were that Mary's health was suffering and the return to Tutbury was having a serious effect on her that summer, and this was posing a lethal threat with winter coming on.

Tutbury was certainly no longer suitable. Mary's rooms were far worse in 1585 than they had been in 1569. Then she had been kept in good rooms with two chambers 24 feet above ground level with windows overlooking Tutbury town. Paulet realised the windows and a latrine could be used to escape, so on her return she was put in a bedchamber immediately under the roof made of timber - she complained of cold and draughts - with no windows looking over the town. The windows looked into the courtyard. Complaints in her letters about her accommodation largely stem from this later period, and an obvious down side of a tighter security system was that psychologically and physically Mary deteriorated. The rigid systems Paulet had in place were risking her health.

The French government protested, showing that despite their failure to get letters to Staffordshire - they were piling up in their London Embassy - they had a contact inside Tutbury and were well informed about conditions.

The challenge to Walsingham

Paulet's tight regime at Tutbury meant that Walsingham was as cut off from the Catholic underground as Mary was. Isolation did not reduce the threat of plots and Walsingham's ability to track threats was limited - he had no police force and limited resources for surveillance. Walsingham's challenge was to re-open a communication channel which Mary had to believe was secure while it was open to scrutiny by the government. How to do this without alerting the conspirators was a massive challenge, and led to a legendary episode in the history of counter espionage -what I will call the Brewers Sting. On the surface, however, moving to a new and more isolated place where Mary could be watched closely had nothing to do with espionage and everything to do with her survival.

Elizabeth's ministers knew another winter in Tutbury could be fatal. On September 13th Walsingham wrote to Paulet that Elizabeth "doubting (not) that the coldness of Tutbury Castle may increase (Mary's) sickness thinks it right she should be removed to some other place, and hearing that Chartley, the Earl of Essex's house, isboth large and strong, in respect that it is environed with water, she would have you see it and certify how you like it".[107]

This importance of this passage cannot be underestimated. On the surface it is simply about security and Mary's health - Elizabeth knew and approved Chartley - in 1575 she had visited there to meet the mistress of the manor, her cousin Lettice, wife of the Earl of Essex. And she was right that Tutbury could be fatal. If these were the arguments that swayed the Queen in favour of Chartley, they were perfectly sufficient. However it is highly likely that for Walsingham the key advantage of the manor was the moat that circled the house. The moat was obviously a security feature,but Walsingham came to see it as offering possibiities for counter espionage. Sometime during 1585 Walsingham had devised a plan to overcome the reluctance of Elizabeth to take action against Mary.

The details are examined in the next section.

Fears for Mary's health if she had to spend the winter of 1585-6 in the damp stinking climate at Tutbury were a good enough excuse to move Mary to Chartley, less than twenty miles away and the home of the Devereux, the Queen's supporters in 1569. The husband of Lettice, Viscount Hereford had rallied to support Huntingdon and Shrewsbury in the crisis of November 1569, and had been created Earl of Essex by Elizabeth as a reward, but was long since dead and the Manor was semi empty as the Countess and her son Robert were no longer living there.

The young Earl of Essex complained about his house being used as a prison, Fraser[108] says Robert Devereux feared Mary would vandalise the house out of hatred of his father for helping move her in 1569 from Tutbury but he was ignored and Mary was moved from Tutbury on Christmas Eve 1585 to the more comfortable and healthier location of Chartley Old Manor. The house could not accomodate as large a party as a mansion like Wingfield, but a house that had coped with Elizabeth 1 could cope with the Scots Queen and her party. The facts dispute any notion that Mary's party was being personally badly treated - certainly they were not half starved. It is worth remembering the Queen did not just drink wine - she washed her face in it.

Using Paulet's accounts, Patrick Collinson calculated that in the months up to her execution her party had consumed- at 1580s prices[109] 353 tuns of beer at a cost of £706, plus 28 tuns of white wine from Gascony costing £480:

A meat bill of £2,279 including 158 carcases of beef, 1341 sheep, 497 calves, 398 lambs, almost a thousand pigs, 1829 lbs of lard, and £617 poultry, pigeons and rabbits. The fish bi, for £1,569, covered 21 codfish, 489 ling, plus samon, turbot, salt eels, white herrings, red herrings, sprats, pike, barbel, chub, tench and perch. Forty gallons of olive oil were needed to dress the salads, and the kitchen in this brief period consumed £20 worth of salt, £15 worth of mustard, and £229 worth of spices.

Chartley suited all parties. The English government had responded to the French Ambassador's complaints about threats to Mary's health, and Mary was no longer in a place she hated. Her recovery in the pastoral valley of Chartley would be steady. While Chartley was even more isolated than Tutbury, visitors were rare anyway and she was close confined with her correspondence tightly controlled.

Chartley was a game changer for Paulet and his colleagues. By January 1586 Paulet was convinced that it was impossible for anyone to "convey a piece of paper as big as my finger" [110] into or out of Chartley so stopping Mary from plotting had been achieved. Black writes that this had made the Castle secure, but by January Mary was in Chartley Manor, and Chartley was the reason Paulet could make the claim. Tutbury Castle could not be put in lockdown - but the Manor with its moat could be made totally secure. Contact with the outside world was sealed off, as the Manor was self sufficient. With one important exception. Chartley Manor did not have a brewhouse to make its own small beer. It would have to import it from Burton on Trent on a weekly basis.

Chapter 9

Catholic Versus Catholic

Walsingham and the role of Chartley in his plans

Elizabeth had forced parliament to make the Act of March 1585 stop short of summary justice, so the authorities needed to have evidence Mary had agreed to the plots of others attempting to kill Elizabeth before she could be put on trial for attempted murder. The Catch 22 of 1572 when Elizabeth refused to take action against her cousin for plotting remained her policy and for Walsingham as spy master this was his core challenge. He approved of the move to Chartley because it helped him tackle his major probem - he did not know whether Mary was in touch with Catholic conspirators.

Walsingham focussed his attention on the ways Mary had sent coded messages abroad. He knew his spy system did not cover all the options. His spy Nicholas Berden reported that Mary was receiving secret letters via a "Ralph Elwes a servant to 'Mr Fenton of Derbyshire'" [111] but the report could not be proved and where the letters came from was not known. Walsingham needed a foolproof way to track letters to and from the exile, to be analysed by Walsingham's secretary and a brilliant codebreaker, Thomas Phelippes (Phillips)

Mary Stuart had long relied on an elaborate system of coded messages in letters sent clandestinely to her agents in Paris notably Thomas Morgan. His link with Mary had been through the French embassy which was still open for business after the Spanish embassy in London closed when Ambassador Mendoza was expelled in

January 1584. From mid 1585 the French ambassador was allowed to write to Mary and vice versa, but Paulet read the letters and stopped any he disliked, while cutting off all other correspondence. The French embassy had been the post box for all continental correspondence but Paulet now refused to accept the letters they sent so letters piled up in the Embassy. However, Walsingham could never be sure that random letters were not getting through as Paulet was not able to ensure laundry women who lived and worked in Tutbury town were not taking letters in and out of the Castle, this being his motive for wanting Mary moved from the summer of 1585.

Chartley, a half timbered manor 8 miles east of Stafford, provided a solution, being both isolated and with a moat, the moat being more than just a security feature. Chartley Manor was smaller than Tutbury and in a shallow valley, with a ruined castle nearby. The Manor had limited facilities, notably lacking a brewhouse. Most aristocrat houses had one, small (low alcohol) beer being a staple of the Tudor diet. The lack of a brewhouse was significant in ways Mary and her party did not grasp until it was too late. Once she was moved on Christmas Eve 1585, Paulet had addressed the problem of the laundry women as Chartley was ideally suited to make the laundry women operate internally. With little population locally, servants had to live in the house and wash laundry in the water supply feeding the moat. They could not live outside as there was no village, this having disappeared before 1500.

Fraser touches on the importance of the moat but sugests that at Chartley the laundry women could move in and out, saying "Paulet himself greatly approved of the change , especially as the amount of water round the house meant that the overspirited laundresses would have less excuse for passing in and out of the gates as they went about their work" [112] In fact they had to work within the manor as unlike Tutbury they had nowhere to go save the local church in nearby Stowe.

Stowe village today, where the church attended by the Devereux stands with its early Tudor tomb of the first Viscount Hereford has the full title of Stowe by Chartley but it would be more realistic to talk of Chartley by Stowe. Stowe is a small village with church and pub. Chartley has no facilities nearby and seems to have had none in 1586. So the laundresses had to do the washing within the enclosure marked by the moat, inside the manor using the water supply for the moat. They could not do the work off site. They could leave the estate to go to the Church at Stowe, but they would be carefully watched to make sure they did not get or give letters. Chartley became a sealed unit. Paradoxically, this was no longer what Walsingham wanted.

Enter Gilbert Gifford

Francis Walsingham knew plotters existed so how could he discover what plans were being made for insurrection? Walsingham had to find ways to convince Mary she had found a way to get letters out, while keeping absolute control of the situation. Unless he could square this circle, the threat Mary posed would continue to fester while the Spanish Armada was being prepared for its lethal mission

In what happened next, Walsingham was aided by divisions within the Catholic community. There was never a simple Protestant-Catholic divide in Elizabethan England, loyalties were fluid and crossover possible. Walsingham needed Catholics prepared to serve the Protestant cause. He succeeded completely, notably with the remarkable Robert Poley/Pooley who penetrated the Babbington Plot, but most successfully with a son of Staffordshire's most famous Catholic family - the Giffard/Gifford family of Chillington near Brewood. Three generations later, the family would save Mary's great grandson Prince Charles after the battle of Worcester by hiding him in the Royal Oak at Boscobel. The historical role of this earlier member of the family played in history has been far less well known, but Gilbert Gifford was the key factor in undermining

Mary's cause in the hall of mirrors that was now developing at Chartley.

The starting point for this remarkable story is Queen Elizabeth's visit to Chillington in 1575 on her only tour of Staffordshire. She visited the Giffords as they had been notably loyal since the Norman Conquest. A Sir John Gifford at the time of Henry VIII had been a favourite of the King and had carried the Royal Banner when the army marched out of Calais to the Battle of the Spurs in 1513. However the family held to the Catholic faith and when Elizabeth found this in 1575 they were summoned before the Privy council, with fines and imprisonment following. In retaliation they sent their son Gilbert to be trained as a Catholic priest abroad, leaving for the continent in 1576. His parents hopes for their son were to be unfulfilled. Gilbert was far from a model student, moved between the two Catholic colleges on the continent and became involved in a fierce argument within Catholicism between an obscure group known as the Secularists and the powerful Jesuit faction, a key reason why he was expelled from the English college in Rome where priests trained.

The Secularists in Rome as trainee priests were not secularists in the modern sense of the word, and were not a religious order as the Jesuits were, and seem to have come initially from Wales.

Apparently they believed most Catholics wanted toleration from the government back home to practice their religion, not confrontation with the protestant regime, arguing the Jesuits were supporting overthrowing the government. The supporters of the Jesuits claimed this was not the case, seeing the action of the English government against their priests as persecution.

Dr William Allen who was trainer of priests in the Catholic seminaries in France and later a cardinal, denied the Jesuits were politically active. In 1581 writing in response to the protestant Anthony Munday he made the notable statement "We put not our trust in princes or practices (schemes, strategems, plots) abroad, nor in arms or forces at home. This is our fight, and for this war, the Society of Jesus (Jesuits TF) and our seminaries were instituted, to this... our priests and students are trained" [113]. It is hard to reconcile this with what he did in the rest of the 1580s, which brought him into conflict with Gilbert Gifford.

Allen was deeply involved in plans for a Spanish led invasion of England and the subsequent government of occupation which would see the Spanish army supporting Mary Stuart as Queen.

He drew up plans for becoming not just Archbishop of Canterbury but also Lord Chancellor, combining religious and political posts if an Armada spearheaded a successful invasion. His long standing support of a Spanish invasion started at least as early as 1576, and he had been in correspondence with Mary since the early 1580s. When Elizabeth's commissioners sought a compromise solution to end her imprisonment as late as 1584 they reported she would not compromise and it is now known she was corresponding with Allen arguing that she could be released from Sheffield by force [114]. Believing that a coup de tat was desirable, Allen threw in his lot with Phillip of Spain which seems to have been the root cause of the conflict with the small group of Catholic emigre priests to be who feared patriotic hostility. But while not agreeing with the Jesuits the emigres did want changes so they could go home, and paradoxically some were prepared for lethal violence against Elizabeth I. Gilbert Gifford was drawn into this dispute.

Despite his sympathy with the Jesuits, Allen was impressed by Gilbert Gifford despite allegations he had caused violence which caused his expulsion from the English college in Rome. Allen was a brilliant college principal who understood talent, and Gilbert Gifford was outstandingly talented. and Allen allowed him back into his French college. It seems Allen had the effect, which the future cardinal certainly did not intend, of turning Gifford into a rebel against a Spanish invasion of England to support Mary Stuart.

The murk of the controversy is impenetrable, but there is no doubt Gifford and his cousin William who was working with Allen at his college at Rheims did not support Allen. Only a specialist historian can fully explain these contradictions which for Gilbert Gifford led him to work with Francis Walsingham.

Lethal plotting

This argument among Catholics on the continent might have been of no wider interest, but the Giffords got to know another trainee priest, John Savage who vowed in their hearing to kill Elizabeth. Fraser has Savage meeting both Giffords and John Ballard, Ballard and Savage later becoming Babington plotters [115] . Gilbert had not said he was opposed to Savage's plans for murder and gained a reputation as willing to help assassinate Elizabeth. His reputation opened the door to Thomas Morgan who certainly wanted to see Elizabeth killed to put Mary on the throne and was linked to Ballard. Perhaps he saw Gifford as the new William Parry turning him too into a potential assassin.

William Gifford his cousin, was a friend of Edmund Grateley, sometime chaplain to the Earl of Arundel, who left Arundel and travelled to Rheims where both were in contact with Thomas Morgan as all three supported the seculars. Morgan asked Dr Gifford to go to England to help counteract Jesuit influence, but William Gifford refused in favour of his cousin Gilbert. Gilbert, who was without a job, took on the mission from Morgan when Grateley suggested he do so. Read suggests Walsingham knew about Grateley and William Clifford [116]. This suggests he knew about Gilbert before his return.

According to Alison Plowden's entry in the Oxford Dictionary of National Biography [117], On 5 April 1585 Gilbert Gifford had been ordained a deacon of the Catholic Church. Later that summerhe left Rheims and direct contact with Dr Allen to go to Paris Sometime in autumn 1585- earlier than December which sometimes is seen as their first meeting - he met Morgan who wrote to Mary mentioning him in a letter of October 5th 1585. Gilbert

Gifford apparently convinced Morgan he could help relieve Mary's isolation, though a precise plan is not mentioned in this letter from Morgan which passed through Philippe's hands, Thomas Philippes as Walsingham's code breaker therefore knew about Gifford and must have told Walsingham a promising character was to enter Mary's service. Morgan wrote to Mary [118] that Gifford was known to him, his father John was a religious prisoner and he was related to the Throckmortons. Significantly, Morgan wrote "John has a brother Robert living within ten miles of her place of captivity" - which was Tutbury at the time - this an uncle presumably was well placed to give Gilbert a base for operations in 1586. Robert Gifford did not play any significant role in what followed even if he did know and approve of what his nephew was doing, but having a base close to Tutbury would have been valuable for his nephew.

The letter puts an ominous slant on Gifford's motives, namely "Present commodity and promise of preferment will weigh much with him...the said Gilbert is instructed how to send her letters to his hand." (also 118) Gifford probably was open to lucrative job offers, as his lack of finance was patently obvious, but he was not just looking for a job when he returned to England. How Morgan suspected Gifford could serve the cause of Mary Stuart is left open in this letter, which urged caution in using this very loose cannon. Clifford would always be unreliable, given that only someone living on the edge of normal morality would be willing to take the risks of breaking open the communication lockdown which had led the French Embassy to have months of undelivered letters. Morgan felt Gifford could solve the problem, but warned Mary he was a risk. The warning was not heeded. As this letter is dated October 5th, it proves Gifford was offering to work for Mary Stuart in early autumn. How he had come to know about the problems of sending letters to Mary in Tutbury is unknown, and Walsingham's hand was probably massaging the course of events.

Walsingham certainly knew and exploited the secularist v Jesuit conflict dividing the emigre Catholic forces, Gifford might have been known to the spymaster before arriving back to England in late 1585. It is almost impossible to see how anyone else could have set up what I call the **Brewers Sting**, and Walsingham found him an ideal ally through the next critical and turbulent months.

Morgan gave Gifford a letter of approval for Mary and the French embassy in London. On arrival in England, Gifford was arrested at Rye and interrogated by Walsingham, and is usually thought to have been turned by Walsingham though he may already have been a double agent, so murky is his past. Alison Plowden argues that [119] "Gifford may or may not have already been employed by Walsingham's secret service, but from this point there can be no doubt about his double dealing". While we have no evidence on Gifford and the world of espionage before meeting Walsingham, he played fair with the spymaster, admittedly partly as it suited him financially. From Walsingham's viewpoint he was entirely satisfactory and was paid accordingly. Gifford was actually on double wages. From the Marian viewpoint he was penniless and needed financial support, so Morgan in France also paid him.

What motivated him to operate so effectively to destroy Mary Stuart is inexplicable bur he fitted what Walsingham wanted like a glove The plan that emerged from their meeting on December 20th 1585 was the Sting. Whether this complex plot was the result of forethought or improvised when Walsingham met Gifford cannot be established. The paradox is that the spymaster was doing a deal with a dubious Catholic plotter who had recently been discussing with John Savage how to kill Elizabeth 1. Why Gifford diverted is unknown but he was the asset Walsingham needed. Whatever motivated Gifford, the reasons Walsingham put his trust in him are clear to see. Only he could operate the Brewers's Sting.

The Sting was an arrangement to enable correspondence to move into and out of Chartley Manor despite its sealing from the outside world. The Game Changer was the fact that the household imported small (ie low alcohol) beer weekly by the barrel load. Antonia Fraser estimates that an English population of 4 million people consumed 18 million barrels of beer each year [120] and the fact that beer had to be imported from Burton, with the increased numbers now in the house, meant a regular trip to bring a full barrel in and an empty barrell out every week. The regular movement of the brewer meant he was largely unnoticed and a deal was struck involving Gifford, known as "the Party" [121] and the Brewer known as "The honest man" [122]- sarcastically as he demanded high pay for his services and silence - to run a postal service via a hollowed out bung into which letters could be fitted. Incoming mail went into a full barrel at Burton, Outgoing mail into the empty barrel leaving Chartley for Burton. The system extended to London and took mail inbound from the French Embassy via Gifford to Burton and the Brewer and then to Mary at Chartley. Outbound the route simply reversed.

The operation of the 'Sting'

Once Walsingham and Gifford had come to an agreement, Phelippes was sent to Chartley to set up the operation while Gifford, bearing his letter from Morgan and his reputation as a Catholic dissident, went to the French Embassy where the letters had piled up to offer to take them into the Manor. However the diplomats having heard Gifford talk were suspicious of him.. The stories that he told did not add up, and they knew he was staying with Phelippes, Walsingham's most trusted aide,. Conyers Read states they did not send any significant correspondence on the first trip to Chartley.

Read [123] says that on 12th January 1586 Gifford went to the embassy and described to the diplomats around Chateauneuf, who had replaced the previous Ambassador, his plan for the system of using the Brewer's barrell . Naturally he ommitted to say Phelippes had set it up - but the diplomats knew he was staying with Phelippes and were so suspicious that they gave Gifford only a letter of recommendation stating nothing of significance and

Thomas Morgan's similar letter. This caution was sensible. Gifford delivered them to the Brewer and they arrived with the Queen four days later.

How Mary knew they were coming is a mystery. The statement by John Cooper that "the plan that Gifford put to her on 16th January 1586 was both more daring and more simple" is wrong in thinking Mary met Gifford. Chartley was locked down - Gifford may have met her secretaries away from Chartley but there was no way he could meet Mary herself with Chartley sealed from visitors [124] . Gifford would not be let in and the Queen was not let out. But the message arrived and Mary, still in her sickbed, was overjoyed: and made Gifford her courier without checking his background. Had the Queen asked her aides to make even elementary checks, what then happened would have taken a different course. Even a check with his Staffordshire relations - of what Gifford had been doing on the continent - possible if he had an uncle nearby - was something her servants could do and could have been illuminating. Mary Stuart disasterously took Gifford at face value.

Once Gifford had the coded material, he took the documents to Thomas Phelippes When speed was needed, Phelippes went to Chartley to translate. It is one of the paradoxes of the story that the only description we have of his appearance is by Queen Mary herself, who saw him at Chartley and knew he was Walsingham's secretary, but had no idea why he was visiting this remote part of the world. When Phelippes had translated the coded message, the envelope went to the wax sealer, Arthur Gregory. Neither at Chartley nor in the French Embassy did anyone ever spot the envelopes had been tampered with. Walsingham is accused of setting up both assassination plots, but the issue is the Brewer's Sting, which Mary accepted with astonishing naivety. Although Antonia Fraser blames the effects of her long confinement, she also shows that Mary accepted Gifford and his agent without any checks at all [125]. Why did Mary use a system without asking questions about its origin? Was the Queen trapped in a false conspiracy set up by Elizabeth's agents or was it was possible to see the dangers of using the system which was too good to be true - as the brighter of her two secretaries, Claude Nau, seems to have grasped?

After two months had convinced both Mary's party and Walsingham's team the system worked, in March 1586 Mary sent a new code to the French Ambassador, the Baron de Chateauneuf to replace codes she suspected had been cracked. Morgan still used the Embassy as the post box from Paris. Mary was sadly unware the brewer gave the codes to Gifford who gave then straight to Phelippes. The codes, no matter how sophisticated, could not provide the security Mary wanted, and she had made a classic espionage mistake. She knew that Walsingham could obtain and decode her letters, so believed a strengthened code would prevent him reading the material.

Simon Singh in his book on codes argues "Both Mary and Babington wrote explicitly about their intention because they believed their communications were secure... the correct use of a strong cipher is a clear boon to sender and reciever, but the misuse of a weak cipher can generate a very false sense of security" [126]. However their failure is more to do with overconfidence in the communication system than the codes being used. It depended on a man, Gifford, who none of the conspirators knew in depth or was examined as to his motives. The outcome would be disasterous . But in Spring 1586 there was nothing in the messages sent that changed the big picture. Walsingham could only wait and see what would come through the system that summer.

Chapter 10

A Staffordshire tragedy

The Babington Plot

If Spring 1585 was a time when Queen Mary could feel she had lost control of her fate, a year later she was recovering both physically and emotionally. Receiving secret coded messages from her supporters convinced her that at last she might be rescued with all her hopes fulfilled. The tragedy was that she did not know that her letters were being read by Elizabeth's agents .Yet this might not have proved the stepping stone to trial and execution had it not been for the conspiracy known as the Babington plot, which took shape in London and Paris and only when apparently ripe for decisive action involved Mary at Chartley.

The paper trail of evidence left by the plotters of 1586 will always be controversial as it depends on spies reports, recollections of conversations among gentry activists, and testimony in trials where torture had been a factor - and above all the crucial correspondence only exists as copies, the originals having been destroyed, which is always standard espionage practice once read. In this case because the letters were passed through government hands, copies were made - which preserves the letters but in a form open to dispute. Yet while it can be accepted much of the Plot was the tavern talk of a group of young Catholic men, the core of the Babington plot was worked out by activists who could plausibly argue for a four stage plan as invented by Ridolfi and which would have continental backing.

This would begin with an assault on Mary's prison to free her before the Bond of Association troops could kill her , involving 100 men, and simultaneously an assassination of Elizabeth by a squad of half a dozen killers This would lead to a 1569 style uprising, with the rebels taking over the government. Finally a foreign - ie Spanish - invasion would secure the country as a whole. How effectively this was planned is doubtful, but assassination was realistic, for both Queens.

Aiming to kill Queen Elizabeth 1 and free Mary Stuart was very high risk, putting the Queen of Scots in danger and likely to spark a Bond of Association backlash. Mary, the Spanish King Phillip II and all experienced observers realised that the attempt to rescue her could go badly wrong - as the rebels of 1569 seem to have realised by scouting and then abandoning an attempt to storm Wingfield Manor with a score of troops - but whether the new plotters understood this is far from clear. They were not experienced in armed conflict and there is no evidence of effective preparation. It is partly for this reason that it has been argued the plot was largely manufactured by Walsingham and his spies, and posed no threat to Elizabeth 1.

Claims that the plot was ramshackle were made by both Antonia Fraser and Charles Nicholl in detailed studies concluding it was not a serious proposition, Fraser describing it as a "gossamer plot" [127]. Charles Nicholl, approaching from the different making angle of activities in the London underworld in which Robert Poley was a key operative for Francis Walsingham, claimed the 1586 plot was "a classic piece of Walsingham 'projection' .... conjured up for political expediency" [128].Yet the men with violence on their mind were real, catholic activists who eventually convinced Mary at Chartley. Walsingham did not invent any of the substance of the plot.

Francis Walsingham may not have known about the original plans to murder Elizabeth, which revolved around John Savage. As an exile Catholic trainee priest in Rheims he discussed with the Giffords his desire to kill Elizabeth 1. But on the continent Savage was harmless. It was when he abandoned the priesthood and returned from the continent to study at the Inns of Court in London that he became a concern to Walsingham. However Savage was no planner and a sharper mind was needed to produce the plot, but Walsingham did not create the plot. He did however know most of what was happening, tracking it through spies.

The planner was John Ballard, a Catholic priest who was a committed rebel. According to Robert Hutchinson [129], he had become a priest on 4th March 1581 being arrested and imprisoned in the Gatehouse Jail, Westminster. There he met another priest Anthony Tyrrell. They escaped and went to Rome, and when Tyrrell returned he was on the fringe of the Plot, observing Ballard's undoubted drive to regicide, about which he was to inform Burghley. Ballard rather than Babington is the real leader, to Charles Nicholl, who claims Anthony Babington was "an amateur, and the plot that bears his name not so much because he was its prime mover, but because he was its weak link. The real animus was the militant, somewhat megalomanic priest Father John Ballard" who brought Babington to the sticking point [130].

Nicholl is right that Babington was an amateur, but wrong that Ballard was the leader. The plot is Babington's because though he did not invent it, he was the connection with Mary at Chartley. And he was the charismatic figure who attracted upwards of a score of Catholic gentlemen to support Ballards' scheme.

For Nicholl the first meeting of the rebels was at the Plough Inn, Temple Bar in March 1586, without Savage or Gifford but with both Ballard and Babington present. Poley was yet to make an appearance. The leader was Sir Anthony Babington, a Derbyshire squire and former page for the Earl of Shrewsbury, when he had worked carrying letters for Mary at Sheffield. His Catholicism had a militant background. His greatgrandfather, Lord Darcy, had been executed for supporting the Pilgrimage of Grace. In 1580 on a trip to Paris he had been recruited by Thomas Morgan and Archbishop Beaton as a courier for Mary Stuart. He found this too dangerous and after marrying and having a daughter abandoned conspiracy, but was targeted by John Ballard, who knew Savage had vowed to kill Elizabeth but needed a key figure with a following, as Savage had no credibility as a leader.

Babington was wealthy and charismatic with a circle of Catholic friends who looked to him as leader. He plausibly explained to his followers that he had plans to summon up half a dozen men to kill Elizabeth while another 100 rode to Chartley to storm the manor and free Mary. Mary would require foreign support, and so Ballard went to France and gained promises of Spanish support from Catholic exile Charles Paget and Spanish Ambassador in Paris, Bernadino de Mendoza, who was still smarting from having been expelled from London when Ambassador. But he did not have authority to promise military support. As with the rebels of 1569 waiting for an invading force at Hartlepool which had not even set sail, Mendoza and Ballard were offering an empty package.

Ballard was not alone, he went to France with a fixer, Bernard Maude [131] who had obtained false passports, came back with Ballard to London on May 22nd and then went to visit Catholics in the north. Ballard did not know Maude was an agent of Walsingham, reporting on what Ballard was doing. The information could have led to the nipping of the plot in the bud, but other priorities ruled. Walsingham was seeking a root and branch solution, not dealing with threats ad hoc. An individual or a group would at some point succeed in using Mary for rebellion, and as this was Ballard's aim, Walsingham's was to use his plot to remove Mary as an inspiration for Catholics to rally round.

Ballard returned at the end of May to tell Babington there was a foreign force of 60,000 men being assembled with the French Guise Catholics and the Spanish having promised an invasion - Babington did not know Madrid was not ready to launch the

Armada and that French promises were pure invention- but was impressed when Ballard said that he had arranged a killer of Elizabeth; "the instrument is Savage and he has vowed to perform it" [132], Babington was still indecisive, as was Savage. Neither would act without the support of Mary Stuart, who knew nothing about their plans, this activity being unknown in the sealed Manor at Chartley.

Walsingham knew the plot was London based, and intensified his monitoring of the plotters via inserting Robert Poley into the inner circle. Poley was unknown till June 1586 in Babington's circle, but rapidly became not just chief confidant, but his link with Walsingham. Poley insinuated himself into Babington's inner circle and arranged three meetings between Babington and his employer, Francis Walsingham. It is almost inconceiveable that an intelligence chief met a potential royal assassin three times, and let him go, but this is what happened. The spy chief's priority was not stopping this plot, but removing Mary. He could have stopped the plot, but he would then have had to track other plots involving Mary, so the objective was always catching Mary. Walsingham wanted her removed once and for all.

Mary and the plot

Savage needed to know Mary approved before he would set out a clear plan for the lethal business of Regicide. The big issue was whether Queen Mary now favoured killing Elizabeth 1. Walsingham wished devoutly she would writea statement to this effect. Walsingham was gambling dangerously - he certainly did not want to trigger an attempt to have Elizabeth murdered. Facilitating a murder plan could go badly wrong - but, for totally different motives, both sides needed Mary Stuart to approve a plot which in the spring of 1586 did not yet exist. She was brought into the reckoning only in July 1586.

In the spring of 1586 Mary had no idea any plans were being laid, and only knew Babington as a pageboy for the Earl of Shrewsbury years earlier. She had greater awareness of Father Ballard and recieved correspondence, which Walsingham was of course reading, telling her that Ballard was in Paris encouraging the Catholic powers to produce an invasion. But whatever Ballard told her was not a reason for Walsingham to act as Elizabeth was not going to take action unless there was an explicit threat to her life. And the actual messages in the brewer's pipeline in the spring of 1586 were less than threatening.

The queen was exploring foreign intervention, having no idea domestic Catholic plotting had revived. Mary was in touch with Mendoza who as Spanish Ambassador in Paris believed that a Spanish invasion was an immediate prospect, the wish being the father to the thought. On 20th May 1586 Mary wrote from Chartley to Mendoza saying she intended to make a will ceding her right to the English throne to Phillip of Spain as a Catholic succession would come through him [133] . This would have been a futile gesture and Mary never made such a will, but the gesture showed that Mary had given up on her son inheriting the English throne even before the Treaty of Berwick effectively abandoned her. If its aim was to encourage the Spanish to invade it was useless, and the will was not made. Until the Spanish naval authorities were ready the Armada was not moving whatever encouragement Mary gave Phillip. This empty promise only shows how few real cards Mary had to use. But she was about to have the prospect of domestic support dangled before her. Support from English rebels was essential if she were to be snatched away from the Bond of Association forces.

In April 1586 Morgan wrote a letter approving Babington as a contact. Walsingham had of course read Morgan's letter, but did not pass it through the Brewer's barrel as he was reluctant to connect Babington and Mary and potentially starting a plot to kill Elizabeth. However Robert Poley monitoring the plotters told him that Babington and his key allies, Titchbourne (the poet), Salesbury and Barnewell were discussing the lawfulness of tyrannicide (regicide). With the plotters discussing the theory of murdering the Queen, [134] there was every chance they would put theory into practice. In June Walsingham released the letter to Gifford for the Brewer to see what Mary Stuart would make of Morgan's approval of Babington

Mary recieved two letters almost simultaneously recommending Anthony Babington. One from Nau's brother in law Fontenay merely told her a dispatch from Scotland was lodged at Babington's house, the other, from Thomas Morgan vouching for Babington. This would be the trigger to action, but in the first instance Mary merely wrote to Babington asking for the missing correspondence. However the action of Morgan in vouching for Babington, as with his reccomendation of Gifford, raised the stakes.

The Queen wrote asking for the Scottish dispatch.[135] This established contact with Babington at last, showing Walsingham that Babington was trusted by Mary. This letter sent on June 25th was enough to push Babington off the fence and commit him to rescuing Mary, which he had been reluctant to do till hearing from the Queen. He replied with more than the missing correspondence - Babington wrote back giving full details of what was intended, crucially specifying "the dispatch of the usurping competitor" - ie murder of Elizabeth by six men- and rescue of Mary from Chartley by Babington himself and a hundred armed men. The correspondence was carefully read by Walsingham and Phelipes who held their breath waiting Mary to reply. Mary recieved Babbington's letter on 14th July. On July 17 after asking her French secretary Nau is advice - he told her to leave Babington's letter unanswered, but was ignored - she wrote back, approving the scheme. [136]

The letter was composed by Mary in French dictated to Nau, then translated into English and coded by English secretary Curle as Babington used English for ciphers. It has been endlessly controversial, with a constant theme that the letter quoted at her trial - the letter of July 17th - was not in her own handwriting

[137] There will never be a version of the crucial letter in her own handwriting as she did not write her own letters and even if she had abandoned her practice of dictating her letters, in this case, she ordered the letter to be destroyed as is standard practice in espionage. It is only because Phelippes copied the letter for Walsingham that we have a copy - though Phelippes clouded affairs by adding his own postscript.

Mary approved killing her cousin, not in so many words but as a key task that had to be carried out, and stated she must know immediately the deed had been done, to prevent Paulet knowing first and killing her. She wrote that Babington would need "an army, or in some very good strength" [138]. When Phelippes read this he drew a gallows on the envelope before sending the translation to Walsingham. At this point a step was taken which has cast doubt on the validity of the letter - Phelippes added a postscript asking for the names of the key conspirators. He then forwarded the letter to Babington via Gifford.

This has reinforced arguments that the plot was faked by the government. The plot was genuine but Walsingham wanted to be able to pick up all the key players - he wanted a clean sweep with no random assassins left free. This was understandable, but foolish as the request for names was clearly spurious. Mary did not need to know the names of the proposed killers. The practical effect of Mary taking the step she had always avoided before and accepting that Elizabeth was to be murdered was to trigger her arrest and trial. Once the 'gallows' letter was deciphered, Queen Mary's fate was sealed.

The crucial point is that Mary accepted Babington's plan for 6 men to murder Elizabeth. By accepting that Elizabeth was to be executed, she crossed the line she had always been careful not to cross before and triggered her trial and execution. Two writers sympathetic to her make this clear. Antonia Fraser briefly but pointedly writes "it was clear to the recipients of her letters - as it was to Walsingham - that the design of which she wrote, and thus tacitly accepted, was that same design of which they too had written, the assassination of the English queen". [139]

John Guy writes "Mary's meaning is perfectly clear. she had consented to Elizabeth's assassination and a foreign invasion. Strictly, she had not specified what the work of the six gentlemen was to be, but the letter from Babington to which she was replying included the graphic passage 'there be six noble gentlemen... who for the zeal they bear to the Catholic cause and your Majesty's service will undertake that tragical execution'". When the two letters are read together, Mary's complicity in the plot is undeniable". [140] It is notable that Royal supporters were muted in defending Queen Mary when she was arrested. Her son failed to do so, as breaking the Treaty of Berwick would have been the result. He had a very bad conscience when he became James I and VI and built his mother a fine tomb. The Catholic powers encouraged their followers to think she was a martyr, but the cynical view of Philip II of Spain was that he was entitled to be English King but he would step aside for his daughter Isabella. Mary he had always expected to have executed once the Armada sailed - he had never put any store in Mary becoming Queen [141]. The French had also long since written her off, Guy, usually sympathetic, accurately comments "Catherine de Medici and her son Henry III by now regarded her as a dangerous embassassment: she simply had to go".[142]

Walsingham had the gallows letter on July 19th. Gifford immediately saw that the end of the game was afoot and fled to the continent on July 20th, aware his role would become public knowledge. He would never return to Staffordshire, though in fact Walsingham was able to keep his name concealed in the trial at Fotheringhay , and in the Continental inquests Thomas Morgan would not testify to Gifford's role in Mary's downfall. But all knew about it. The French Ambassador Chateauneuf wrote laconically in his report to the French King "The Queen of Scots and her principal servants placed great confidence in the said Gifford.... and thence came the ruin of the said Queen". [143]

There was a great deal more to the ruin of Mary Queen of Scots than trusting Gilbert Gifford. Perhaps Morgan would not testify in Catholic France when questions were asked about his role because he knew it was his uncritical recommendation that had convinced the French Embassy and Mary in Chartley to give Gifford control of the correspondence. Without Gifford the Brewer's sting could not have worked, and it suited him to serve Walsingham faithfully. He undoubtedly served the interest of those who defended Elizabeth Tudor and sought to bring Mary Stuart's activities to an end. Why remains a mystery, but his record caused his parents deep grief. John Gifford had suffered for his faith, and Phelippes was in contact with him throughout the Brewer's Sting, though the father had no idea what his son was doing. Now he had discovered sending his son to be a priest had led to the fatal developments consuming the woman he thought of as the rightful Queen of England, his cup of bitterness overflowed. He wrote to Phelippes the bitterest of letters, saying "I have written to my unfortunate son. I would God he had never been born".[144]

That a Staffordshire man should play so crucial a role has a poetic logic, and Gifford's role in Mary's downfall was vital but it was certainly not the trigger. Ultimately it was Babington's willingness to plot the killing of Elizabeth 1 and Mary's acceptance of this which was decisive.

The last days at Chartley

Mary final two months in Staffordshire had aspects of Greek Tragedy. As the summer developed, the exiled Queen believed the bleak midwinter had been replaced by a summer of promise. She was recovering physically and emotionally, and on June 3rd she was carried out of doors to watch duck hunting. She would soon be strong enough for horse riding. It was with this renewed energy that she responded to Babington. She had no idea Walsingham and his associates knew what she was planning.

Mary was now up and about at Chartley Manor, allowing a belated spring clean and Paulet proposed she move to Tixall Manor, three miles away. The taciturn Paulet invited her to watch a deer hunt, and she rode on horseback for the last time in her life. She had recovered so much that she rode ahead of Paulet, and stopped to let him catch up.[145] The final moments have already been accounted for.

After her arrest, she and her party were taken back to the house of Sir Walter Aston at Tixall while her rooms at Chartley were searched for evidence to present at her trial. On 25th August she was brought back to Chartley, telling beggars at the gate of Tixall she had nothing to give them. On 5th September Paulet was ordered to confiscate her money and isolate her from her servants, which Walsingham protested was an over reaction.[146] Guy suggests Walsingham feared Mary would sicken and die - and that this was what Elizabeth wanted to avoid trial and execution. Paulet and Richard Bagot, a local magistrate, close friend of the Devereux family and committed protestant entered the Queen's bedroom and took her reserve of money, put aside for rewarding her servants, against her fierce protests The orders certainly came from Elizabeth, holed up in the fortress of Windsor Castle and suffering shock after learning of so detailed a plot against her. To make Mary's feelings even more bitter, she found her son, while opposing her execution, had the only option to make his protests meaningful was to break the Treaty of Berwick in protest and remove the alliance with England. He did not do so. The final stage of her time at Chartley was marred by foolish cruelty to her servants, and was driven by vindictiveness of a monarch and her ministers traumatised by how an element of Catholicism had degenerated into detailed plotting murder and destruction. But Mary's servants at Chartley had not been responsible. The low point was the failure to allow a priest to baptise the child of her secretary, Curle. Mary acted as priest using Catholic rites.[147] Curle, already imprisoned, was kept in prison for a year, while Nau, the French secretary who co-operated, was housed by Walsingham.

Mary was taken to Fotheringhay castle for her trial on September 21st. Her illnesses had returned. Chartley had been good for her, helping to regain her spirits and strength, but the outcome of her visit had been disasterous. Unlike Buxton, she gave no sign she regretted leaving the County. She now had more vital issues to focus on than where she was imprisoned. When she left the county, Staffordshire's role in her story lapsed into obscurity. Tixall Manor was demolished leaving only the splendid gatehouse that Mary would certainly have seen, even if unfinished. Chartley Old Manor burned down in 1781. Only Tutbury Castle, a pale shadow of the major fort it had been when the Queen was kept there, remains in some ways a monument to her captivity. The personnell, warriors, plotters, politicians, laundresses and players in plot and counter plot have vanished leaving little record.

There are no ghosts from this story anywhere in the parts of Staffordshire, Tutbury, Chartley and Tixall, that Mary Stuart visited. The personalities involved in the captivity of Mary Queen of Scots when they were in Staffordshire have come to be seen as figures with no context or location. Mary and her people - and passed through this relatively remote part of the country without leaving much trace save at Tutbury. Paulet is today only seen as a brutal jailer - unfair and misleading - his honorable refusal to murder Mary in cold blood at Elizabeth's request, is a blot on Elizabeth's record which is muted in most books about Elizabeth, viewing her character through the lens of her own propaganda devised in the Gloriana cult of the 1590s.[148] Paulet's stand deserves to be brought back into focus as part of clearing away the many myths about Mary's time in Staffordshire.

Locally, it is often remembered that the exiled Queen was captive at Chartley, but believed to have been kept in the Castle not the Manor where she was actually kept: though the Manor was visited by two Queens, and places Elizabeth 1 visited are not normally easily forgotten. Even the role Tutbury played in the historical record in 1569 has been the victim of the victor's writing of history. Mary could have been captured by the Catholic rebels if they had acted quicker, and history could have taken a leap. Whatever historical speculation suggests in the debates which continue indefinitely, there is no doubt that Staffordshire's places played a key role in her tragic story of captivity and plotting. Important people lived here and what happened in these places deserves to be remembered.

Bibliography

Oxford Dictionary Of National Biography (DNB)

Duke of Norfolk - Michael A R Graves 03 01 2008

Gilbert Gifford/Giffard - Alison Plowden23 09 2004

Mary Stewart/Stuart 1542-87 - Julian Goodacre 24 05 2007

Ackroyd Peter History of England Vol II, THE TUDORS, Pan Books 2013

Alford Stephen THE WATCHERS Penguin 2013

Andrews Anne A HISTORY OF TIXALL 1 Tixall's Churches, Hanyards Press 1995

Bardon Papers, ed Conyers Read, Royal Historical Society 1909

Calendar of State Papers (Scotland) 1585-86 (CSP 1585-6)

Collinson, Patrick THE ENGLISH CAPTIVITY OF MARY QUEEN OF SCOTS, Sheffield History Pamphlets, Sheffield, 1987

Cooper, John THE QUEEN'S AGENT, Faber & Faber, 2011/2012- *Francis Walsingham at the Court of Elizabeth 1,* Pegasus Books New York, 2013, *Sir Francis Walsingham and the Rise of Espionage in Elizabethan England.* page numbers identical.

Fletcher Anthony & MacCulloch Diarmaid, TUDOR REBELLIONS, 5th ed. Pearson-Longman 2004.

Fraser Antonia, MARY QUEEN OF SCOTS Phoenix Press 2002.

Guy John 2004 MY HEART IS MY OWN, Fourth Estate 2004

Guy John 2016 ELIZABETH THE FORGOTTEN YEARS Penguin 2016

Hutchinson, Robert ELIZABETH'S SPYMASTER, (Walsingham TF) Phoenix 2007

Jenkins Elizabeth ELIZABETH AND LEICESTER, Panther 1972

Kesselring, KJ THE NORTHERN REBELLION OF 1569, Palgrave-MacMillan 2007

Lynch, Michael ED MARY STEWART, Basil Blackwell 1988

Greengrass M 1988 *IN Lynch 1988* MARY, DOWAGER QUEEN OF FRANCE

Holmes P J 1988 *In Lynch 1988* MARY STEWART IN ENGLAND

Cowans Ian B 1988 *In Lynch 1988* THE ROMAN CONNECTION

MacCaffrey, Wallace T THE SHAPING OF THE ELIZABETHAN REGIME Princeton 1968

Nicholl, Charles THE RECKONING *The Murder of Christopher Marlowe* Vintage 2002

Oxford History of England, Black J B, 1959 Vol 8 the Reign of Elizabeth, 2nd Edition, Clarendon Press (OUP Oxford University Press)

Oxford, New History of England, Penry Williams, 1995, the later Tudors, England 1547-16

Read Conyers, MR SECRETARY WALSINGHAM, 3 Vols, Archon Books 1967. (Original The Clarendon Press, The Clarendon Press (Oxford University Press) 1925)

Singh, Simon THE CODE BOOK Fourth Estate 2000

Transactions of the Royal Historical Society 12 (2002), Geoffrey Parker , The Prothero Lecture - read 4th July 2001.

Watkins Susan MARY QUEEN OF SCOTS, Thames & Hudson, 2001

Williams Gareth et al TUTBURY A CASTLE FIRMLY BUILT Oxford, Archaeopress, 2011.

Williams Kate RIVAL QUEENS Hutchinson 2018

Wormald Jenny, MARY QUEEN OF SCOTS A study in Failure, George Philip 1988, John Donald 2017

Endnotes

1 In this book this spelling will be used as 'John Guy (1)John Guy and Antonia Fraser both use this spelling.

2 Jenny Wormald MARY QUEEN OF SCOTS A Study in Failure 2017

3 The account is taken from John Guy, 2004, pp484-485 and Antonia Fraser 2002, pp613-615. Both are based on the writing of Dominique Bourgoing, her physician, who wrote an account of the last seven months of her life

4 Guy 2004 p41, Fraser 2004 pp38-39

5 Guy 2004 p90

6 Guy 2004 pp90-91

7 Guy 2004 p92

8 M Greengrass MARY DOWAGER QUEEN OF FRANCE 1988 p171

9 Ian B Cowans THE ROMAN CATHOLIC CONNECTION 1988 107-8 refers to her ambiguous position.

10 Jenny Wormald 2017 p103

11 Guy 2004 p131

12 Williams Kate 2018 p98, Fraser 2002 p326. Fraser has a damning quote from Mary to Nau

13 Guy 2004 p314

14 Fraser 2002 pp310-320

15 Fraser 2002 p349

16 Fraser 2002 p358

17 Wormald 2017 p167

18 Guy 2004 p314

19 Guy 2004 p322

20   Fraser2002 pp409-412

21   Guy 2004 p368

22   Guy 2004 p369

23   Wormald 2017 pp35-36

24   Fraser 2002 pp517-518

25   Black 1959 p110

26   Williams 2018 pp233-234, Black 1959 p110

27   Williams 2018 p244

28   Fraser 2002 pp480-481

29   Fraser 2002 p516

30   Fraser 2002 p229

31   Guy 2004 p462

32   Ackroyd 2013 Vol II, pp347-348, Jenkins 1972 p177

33   Ackroyd 2013 Vol II p355

34   MacCaffrey 1968 p324

35   Guy 2004 p443

36   Guy 2004 p444

37   Fraser 2002, Knox quote p96

38   Fraser 2002 p547

39   Guy 2004, p443

40   Fraser 2004 pp39-40

41   Fraser 2004 p548

42   Guy 2004 p439

43   Fraser 2002 p511

44   Williams Gareth 2011 p108. The Image is in Watkins 2001, p186

45   Black 1959 p130. Conyers Read, 1909 ppxxii- xxiii. Sources this as CAL Spanish papers 1568-79 p97

46   Fraser 2002, p518

47   Fraser 2002 p521

48   Fraser 2002 p520

49   Fraser 2002 p522

50 PJ Holmes 1988 p200

51 Fraser 2002 p203

52 Norfolk entry - Oxford Dictionary of National Biography Quote from Elizabeth from Camden, Annales

53 Black 1959 p137

54 Fraser 2002 p522

55 Collinson 1987 p40

56 Black 1959 -p134

57 Collinson 1987 p41

58 Kesselring 2007 p49

59 Kesselring 2007 pp58-59

60 Kesselring 2007 p59

61 Kesselring 2007 p61

62 Kesselring 2007 p67

63 Black 1959 pp139-140, Kesselring p76

64 Kesselring 2007 pp76-77

65 Fletcher & MacCulloch 2004 p107

66 Fraser 2002 p526

67 Holmes 1988 p198

68 Fraser 2002 p520

69 Transactions of the Royal Historical Society 2002 p192, note 51

70 Transactions 2002 p193

71 Transactions 2002 p194 note 56

72 Transactions2002 p197

73 Transactions 2002 p204

74 Black 1959 p151

75 Fraser 2002 p531

76 Transactions 2002 p205. The letter to Shrewsbury 5 9 71 is in Collinson 1987 pp42-43

77 Acroyd Vol II, 2013, pp377-378

78   Bardon Papers 1909 have only 3 relevant documents-Summary of charges against Mary pp1-4, Instructions to Lord De La Ware to address the Queen pp5-9, and a petition to the Queen to debar Mary from the succession . Response from Elizabeth Ackroyd Vol II 2013 pp366-7

79   Guy 2004 p470

80   Collinson 1987 p24

81   Wormald 2017 p190, Black 1959 p373

82   Wormald 2017 p194

83   Fraser2002 pp542-543

84   Fraser 2002 p539

85   Guy 2004 p448

86   Fraser 2002 p549

87   Fraser 2002 p562

88   Williams, Kate, 2018 p291

89   Fraser 2002 pp583-584, Guy 2004 pp472-473 has less than a page on the Throckmorton plot. Stephen Alford 2013 has two chapters

90   Fraser 2002, pp583-584

91   Black 1959 p376

92   Ackroyd Vol II, 2013 pp406-7

93   Black 1959 p377, Fraser 2002 p588

94   Fraser 2002 p586

95   Black 1959 p378. Guy has nothing on Parry - Alford 79 index entries and a chapter on his plot.

96   Fraser 2002 p638

97   Fraser 2002 p517

98   Guy 2004 p456

99   Watkins 2001 p176, Fraser 2002 p593

100   Singh 2000 p35

101   Guy 2016 p80

102   102 Fraser op cit p574

103   Black 1959 p370

104   Fraser 2002 p593

105   Hutchinson 2007 p119

106   Fraser 2002 p589

107   Hutchinson 2007 p120

108   Fraser 2002 p596

109   Collinson 1987 pp18-19

110   Black 1959 p379

111   Hutchinson 2007 p119

112   Fraser 2002 p596

113   Alford 2013 p67

114   Black 1959 p376

115   Fraser 2002 p598

116   Read Vol II 1925 p429

117   Plowden Oxford Dictionary of National Biography, Gilbert Gifford entry

118   Calendar of State Papers (Scotland) for 1585-86 pp120-121

119   Oxford Dictionary of National biography, Gilbert Gifford entry

120   Fraser 2002 p593

121   Alford 2013 p198

122   Alford 2013 p205

123   Read Vol III 1925 p10-11, Fraser on the reception of Gifford by the French Embassy 2002 pp599-600

124   Cooper 2012 p210, Fraser 2002 p600

125   Fraser 598-601

126   Singh 2000 p42

127   Fraser 2002 p613

128   Nicholl 2002 p173

129   Hutchinson 2006 p125

130   Nicholl 2002 p174

131   Nicholl 2002 p175-6

132   Nicholl 2002 p176

133 Black 1959 p390

134 Cooper 2012p 216

135 Fraser 2002 pp605-606

136 Fraser 2002 pp607-608

137 Cooper 2012 p218, p225 Babington destroyed Mary's July 17th letter

138 Fraser 2002 p608

139 Fraser 2002 p607

140 Guy 2004 p483

141 Black 1959 p390

142 Guy 2004 p495

143 GUY 2004 PP480-481

144 Alford 2013 p232

145 Fraser 2002 p614

146 Guy 2004 pp485-6

147 Fraser 2002 p617

148 Collinson 1987 p57 - states the letter is from Paulet and Sir Drue Drury, but appears to be from Paulet only.

Printed in Poland
by Amazon Fulfillment
Poland Sp. z o.o., Wrocław